Mathematical Studies
Standard Level

for the IB Diploma

Exam Preparation Guide

Paul Fannon, Vesna Kadelburg,
Ben Woolley, Stephen Ward

CAMBRIDGE
UNIVERSITY PRESS

CONTENTS

INTRODUCTION

ABOUT THIS BOOK

If you are using this book, you're probably getting quite close to your exams. You may have started off as a bright-eyed student keen to explore international perspectives in mathematics and the nature of mathematical knowledge, but now you want to know how to get the best possible grade! This book is designed to revise all of the material that you need to know, and to provide examples of the most common types of exam questions for you to practise, along with some hints and tips regarding exam technique and common pitfalls.

> ⚠️ Any common pitfalls and useful exam hints will be highlighted in these boxes.

> 🖩 This type of box will be used to point out where graphical calculators can be used effectively to simplify a question or speed up your work. Common calculator pitfalls will also be highlighted in such boxes.

> ▶ If the material in a chapter involves maths outside of that chapter, this kind of box will direct you to the relevant part of the book where you can go and remind yourself of the relevant maths.

The most important ideas and formulae are emphasised in the 'What you need to know' sections at the start of each chapter. When a formula or set of formulae is given in the Formula booklet, there will be a book icon next to it 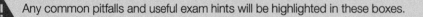. If formulae are not accompanied by such an icon, they do **not** appear in the Formula booklet and you may need to learn them or at least know how to derive them.

For Mathematical Studies Standard Level, each of the written papers:

- is worth 40% of the final grade
- is one and a half hours long (plus 5 minutes of reading time)
- has a total of 120 marks available.

The difference between the two papers is that Paper 1 consists of 15 short questions while Paper 2 consists of 4 or 5 long questions which require you to use and connect several different ideas.

IMPORTANT EXAM TIPS
- **Grab as many marks as you can.**
  - If you cannot do an early part of a question, write down a sensible answer and use that in later parts or, if the part you could not do was a 'show that' task, use the given result. You will still pick up marks.

- Do not throw away 'easy marks':
  - Where appropriate, give units with your answers.
  - Give all answers exactly or to three significant figures, or to the accuracy specified in the question. Each time you fail to do so you will lose a mark.
  - Do not use rounded intermediate values, as this can result in an inaccurate answer; store all intermediate values in your calculator.
  - Read the questions carefully and make sure you have provided the answer requested. For example, if the question asks for coordinates, give both x and y values. If the question asks for an equation, make sure that you have something with an equals sign in it.
  - Do not leave anything blank; you won't be given negative marks for wrong answers, and you may pick up a mark for writing down something sensible.
  - Do not cross out your working unless you have already replaced it with something else.
- **The questions are actually worded to help you.**
  - Make sure you know what each command term means. (These are explained in the IB syllabus.) For example:
    - 'Write down' means that there does not need to be any working shown. So, for this type of question, if you are writing out lines and lines of algebra, you have missed something.
    - 'Hence' means that you have to use the previous part somehow. You will not get full marks for a correct answer unless you explicitly show how you have used the previous part.
    - 'Hence or otherwise' means that you can use any method you wish, but it's a pretty big hint that the previous part will help in some way.
    - 'Sketch' means that you do not need to do a precise and to-scale drawing; however, you should label all the important points and at the very least where the curve crosses any axes.
  - If the question refers to solutions, you should expect to get more than one answer.
  - Look out for links between the parts of a question, particularly in the long questions.
- **Use your 5 minutes of reading time effectively.**
  - Decide on the order in which you will attempt the questions. You do not have to answer them in order and you might want to do questions similar to ones you have seen before first. You will almost certainly want to do some parts of Section B before the last few questions in Section A.
  - Decide which questions can be done easily or checked effectively on the calculator. Do not be surprised if this is the majority of questions.
  - On Paper 2, think about how different parts of a question link together. There is often a difficult part in the middle of the question, but you can skip it and move on to the next part.

⚠ Practise using the reading time when attempting your practice papers.

Most importantly, there is nothing like good preparation to make you feel relaxed and confident going into an exam, which in turn should help you achieve your best possible result.

Good luck!

The author team

1 WORKING WITH NUMBERS

- The definition of the different number sets:
    - $\mathbb{N}$ is the set of natural numbers $\{0, 1, 2, 3, \ldots\}$.
    - $\mathbb{Z}$ is the set of integers $\{\ldots, -3, -2, -1, 0, 1, 2, 3, \ldots\}$; $\mathbb{Z}^+$ is the set of positive integers; $\mathbb{Z}^-$ is the set of negative integers.
    - $\mathbb{Q}$ is the set of all rational numbers. A rational number can be written as a fraction using two integers, where the denominator must not be zero. Examples include $-\dfrac{1}{2}, 0.54, 17, 2\dfrac{3}{4}$.
    - $\mathbb{R}$ is the set of all real numbers. These include the natural numbers, integers and rational numbers, as well as irrational numbers. An irrational number cannot be written as a fraction; examples include π, $\sqrt{3}$, $\sin 60°$.
- Numbers can be written to a fixed number of decimal places or significant figures:
    - To round to one decimal place, look at the digit in the second decimal place; to round to two decimal places, look at the digit in the third decimal place. If that digit is less than 5, round down; if the digit is 5 or more, round up.
    - To round to three significant figures, look at the digit to the right of the third significant figure. If that digit is less than 5, round down; if the digit is 5 or more, round up.
- Very small and very large numbers can be expressed in standard form (or scientific notation) $a \times 10^k$ where $1 \le a < 10$ and k is an integer.
- To find the percentage error, use the formula $\varepsilon = \left| \dfrac{v_A - v_E}{v_E} \right| \times 100\%$, where v_E is the exact value and v_A is the approximate value of v.
- Converting to a larger unit means fewer of them, so divide. Converting to a smaller unit means more of them, so multiply.
- To change one currency to another, multiply by the appropriate exchange rate. When commission is charged, first work out the amount of commission paid. The exchange rate is then applied to the 'original amount – commission paid'.

- The square root of any number that is not a perfect square (e.g. $\sqrt{4}$) or the ratio of two perfect squares (e.g. $\sqrt{\dfrac{16}{25}}$) will be irrational. Many trigonometric ratios (e.g. $\sin 45°$) are irrational.
- Zeros at the beginning of a decimal (e.g. **0.000** 301) and at the end of a large number (e.g. 134 **000**) do not count as significant figures. The first significant figure of a number is the first non-zero digit in the number, counting from the left.

1.1 DIFFERENT TYPES OF NUMBERS

WORKED EXAMPLE 1.1

Write down a number that is:

(a) a real number but not rational

(b) a rational number and in $\mathbb{N}$

(c) a rational number but not in $\mathbb{N}$.

(a) π

> π is an irrational number as it cannot be written as a fraction.

(b) 3

> ⚠ All integers are rational numbers, e.g. $3 = \dfrac{3}{1}$ is a fraction with denominator 1.

(c) $\dfrac{1}{2}$

Practice questions 1.1

1. Mark each cell to indicate which number set(s) the number belongs to. The first row has been completed for you.

	$\mathbb{N}$	$\mathbb{Z}$	$\mathbb{Q}$	$\mathbb{Z}$
-3	✗	✓	✓	✓
0.76				
$\cos 120°$				
$\sqrt{5}$				
1.23×10^8				

2. The Venn diagram shows the sets $\mathbb{N}, \mathbb{Q}, \mathbb{R}$ and $\mathbb{Z}$.

(a) Add labels to show which region corresponds to each set.

(b) Put the following numbers into the correct set:
3, −3, 3.3 and π.

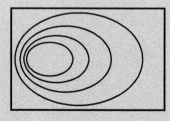

3. A set contains the elements x such that $-4 \le x < 6$, $x \in \mathbb{Z}$. Each element is equally likely to occur. One element is drawn at random.

Find the probability that it is in: (a) $\mathbb{N}$ (b) $\mathbb{Q}$.

1.2 STANDARD FORM AND SI UNITS

WORKED EXAMPLE 1.2

If $x = 2.3 \times 10^{12}$ cm and $y = 4.8 \times 10^{-11}$ km:

(a) write x and y in metres

(b) find xy, giving your answer in metres squared in the form $a \times 10^k$ where $1 \leq a < 10$ and $k \in \mathbb{Z}$.

> ⚠️ 1 km = 1000 m, 1 cm = 0.01 m, 1 mm = 0.001 m
> 1 kg = 1000 g, 1 mg = 0.001 g
> 1 m² = 100 cm × 100 cm = 10 000 cm²
> 1 m³ = 100 cm × 100 cm × 100 cm = 1 000 000 cm³.

(a) $x = \dfrac{2.3 \times 10^{12} \text{ cm}}{100 \text{ cm/m}} = 2.3 \times 10^{10} \text{ m}$

> ⚠️ Converting to a larger unit means fewer of them, so divide. Converting to a smaller unit means more of them, so multiply.

$y = 4.8 \times 10^{-11} \text{ km} \times 1000 \text{ m/km} = 4.8 \times 10^{-8} \text{ m}$

(b) $xy = 2.3 \times 10^{10} \text{ m} \times 4.8 \times 10^{-8} \text{ m}$
$= 1104 \text{ m}^2 \approx 1.10 \times 10^3 \text{ m}^2$

> Make sure that you can convert numbers to standard form on your calculator. However, you must not write calculator notation, such as 10E3, in your answer.

Practice questions 1.2

4. Given that $a = 5.6 \times 10^{10}$ and $b = 1.6 \times 10^{-4}$, calculate the following, giving your answer in the form $c \times 10^k$ where $1 \leq c < 10$ and $k \in \mathbb{Z}$:

(a) ab (b) $\dfrac{a}{b}$

5. Given that $x = 4.3 \times 10^8$ g and $y = 0.98$ hours, calculate $\dfrac{x}{y}$, giving your answer in kg per second in the form $a \times 10^k$ where $1 \leq a < 10$ and $k \in \mathbb{Z}$.

6. A room measures 3.1 m by 4.4 m. Find the area of the room in:

(a) m²   (b) cm²

(c) Give your answer to (b) in the form $a \times 10^k$ where $1 \leq a < 10$ and $k \in \mathbb{Z}$.

> 🖩 If numbers are very big or very small, the GDC gives the answers in standard form automatically.

1.3 APPROXIMATION AND ESTIMATION

WORKED EXAMPLE 1.3

(a) Write down $\sqrt{2}$ correct to two decimal places.

(b) Write down $\sqrt{2}$ correct to the nearest ten.

(c) Write down $\sqrt{2}$ correct to two significant figures.

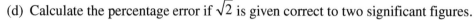
⚠ In an exam question, if a specific degree of accuracy is not asked for, give your answer correct to three significant figures.

(d) Calculate the percentage error if $\sqrt{2}$ is given correct to two significant figures.

(a) 1.41

$\sqrt{2} = 1.41421....$ To round to 2 decimal places, look at the digit in the third decimal place, which is 4. It is less than 5, so round down.

(b) 0

⚠ Remember that 0 is a multiple of ten.

(c) 1.4

Find the second significant figure and look at the digit after it. As 1 < 5, round down.

(d) $\varepsilon = \left| \dfrac{v_A - v_E}{v_E} \right| \times 100\% = \left| \dfrac{1.4 - \sqrt{2}}{\sqrt{2}} \right| \times 100\%$

$= 1.01\%$ (3 SF)

Substitute the rounded value, $v_A = 1.4$, and the exact value, $v_E = \sqrt{2}$, into the formula for percentage error. The modulus sign simply means that we remove any negative sign which occurs.

Practice questions 1.3

7. (a) Write π correct to three decimal places.

(b) Find the percentage error when π is given correct to three decimal places.

8. (a) Write down $\sqrt{46}$ and π correct to three significant figures.

(b) Write down the value of $\pi^{\sqrt{46}}$, giving all the digits shown on your calculator.

(c) Write down the value of $\pi^{\sqrt{46}}$ using the approximate values found in part (a), giving all the digits shown on your calculator.

(d) To how many significant figures is your result in part (c) correct?

(e) What is the percentage error in your answer to part (c)?

1.4 CURRENCY CONVERSIONS

WORKED EXAMPLE 1.4

The table shows the exchange rates for US dollars and euros:

	? USD	? EUR
1 USD	1	0.78
1 EUR	p	1

(a) Find the value of p to two decimal places.

(b) What is the value of $150 in euros?

(c) Jamie changes €300 into dollars. She is charged 6% commission. How many dollars does she receive?

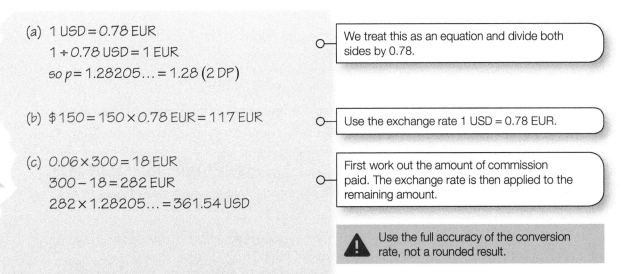

(a) 1 USD = 0.78 EUR

$1 \div 0.78$ USD = 1 EUR

so $p = 1.28205... = 1.28$ (2 DP)

○— We treat this as an equation and divide both sides by 0.78.

(b) $150 = 150 × 0.78 EUR = 117 EUR

○— Use the exchange rate 1 USD = 0.78 EUR.

(c) 0.06 × 300 = 18 EUR

300 − 18 = 282 EUR

282 × 1.28205... = 361.54 USD

○— First work out the amount of commission paid. The exchange rate is then applied to the remaining amount.

⚠ Use the full accuracy of the conversion rate, not a rounded result.

Practice questions 1.4

9. The table gives the conversion rates between British pounds (GBP) and Australian dollars (AUD). Find x, and hence find the number of pounds which can be bought with 1000 AUD if there is a 4% commission.

	? GBP	? AUD
1 GBP	1	1.58
1 AUD	x	1

10. A currency office buys one South African rand (SAR) for 10.95 Japanese yen and sells one SAR for 11.05 yen.

(a) Blaise converts 1000 SAR to yen for a holiday. While on holiday he spends half of this money. On his return he converts the remainder back to SAR. How many SAR will he get back?

(b) Robbie also converts 1000 SAR to yen for a holiday. He then cancels his holiday and changes all the yen back to SAR. How much has Robbie lost after the two transactions? Express your answer as a percentage of Robbie's original 1000 SAR.

Mixed practice 1

1. If $x = 1.23 \times 10^5$ and $y = 1.46 \times 10^{-3}$:

    (a) write y to four decimal places

    (b) calculate xy, giving your answer in decimal form

 'Decimal form' means as an ordinary number.

    (c) calculate $\dfrac{y}{x}$, giving your answer in the form $a \times 10^k$ where $1 \le a < 10$ and $k \in \mathbb{Z}$.

2. Look at this list of numbers:

    $3.14 \times 10^2,\ 100\pi,\ \dfrac{2200}{7},\ \sqrt{100\,000},\ 310$

    (a) Which of these numbers is largest?

    (b) List all the numbers which are members of: (i) $\mathbb{Z}$ (ii) $\mathbb{Q}$.

    (c) What is the largest number of significant figures to which all five numbers are equal?

3. A farmer wants to plant a new forest in a field covering a rectangular area of 3 km by 5 km.

    (a) Find the area of the forest in m², giving your answer in the form $a \times 10^k$ where $1 \le a < 10$ and $k \in \mathbb{Z}$.

    (b) Each tree needs an area of 3.4 m². Find the maximum number of trees which could be planted. Give your answer to the nearest thousand trees.

4. A travel agent converts dollars and yen at an exchange rate of \$1 = 103 yen. They charge 5% commission on all transactions.

    (a) If Dima converts 10 000 yen to dollars, how much will he receive?

    (b) If he converts \$500 to yen, how much will he receive?

5. (a) Write 125.987 in the form $a \times 10^k$ where $1 \le a < 10$ and $k \in \mathbb{Z}$.

    (b) Write 125.987 to two significant figures.

    (c) What is the percentage error when rounding 125.987 to two significant figures?

6. Nicole wants to convert pounds to euros. She can choose between two different offers.

    • Offer 1: an exchange rate of 1 pound to 1.26 euros with no commission.

    • Offer 2: an exchange rate of 1 pound to 1.30 euros with 5% commission.

    Which offer provides Nicole with the better deal?

7. Mark each cell to indicate which number set(s) the number belongs to. The first row has been completed for you.

Number	$\mathbb{N}$	$\mathbb{Z}$	$\mathbb{Q}$	$\mathbb{R}$
-5	✗	✓	✓	✓
0				
$\tan 45°$				
$\tan 60°$				
9.9×10^{24}				
1×10^{-2}				
π				

8. The Earth can be modelled by a perfect sphere with a radius of 6700 km.

(a) Find the volume of the Earth in km^3.

 The formula for the volume of a sphere is given in the Formula booklet.

(b) Find the volume of the Earth in cm^3, giving your answer in the form $a \times 10^k$ where $1 \le a < 10$ and $k \in \mathbb{Z}$.

(c) If the average density of the earth is 6.7 g/cm³, find the mass of the Earth.

Going for the top 1

1. The value of x is quoted as 20 to the nearest 10. The value of y is quoted as 1.6 to two significant figures.

(a) Write an inequality in the form $a \le x < b$ showing the range that x can lie in.

(b) What is the smallest value $3x - 7$ could take?

(c) Find the largest possible percentage error if $\dfrac{x}{y}$ is quoted as being 12.5.

2. The table below shows the values of different currencies compared to one US dollar:

	GBP	CHF	EUR	JPY	AUD
1 USD	0.66	0.97	0.78	102.48	1.02

(a) How many US dollars can you get with one British pound (GBP)?

(b) What is the exchange rate for euros (EUR) to Japanese yen (JPY)?

(c) Camille converts 1000 US dollars to British pounds, then Swiss francs (CHF), then euros, then Japanese yen, then Australian dollars, and then back to US dollars. For each transaction, she pays 5% commission. How much does she have left at the end, to the nearest US dollar?

2 SEQUENCES AND SERIES

WHAT YOU NEED TO KNOW

- The notation for sequences and series:
  - u_n represents the nth term of the sequence u.
  - S_n denotes the sum of the first n terms of the sequence.
- An arithmetic sequence has a constant difference, d, between terms. If the first term is u_1, then:
  - $u_n = u_1 + (n-1)d$
  - $S_n = \dfrac{n}{2}[2u_1 + (n-1)d] = \dfrac{n}{2}(u_1 + u_n)$
- A geometric sequence has a constant ratio, r, between terms:
  - $u_n = u_1 r^{n-1}$
  - $S_n = \dfrac{u_1(r^n - 1)}{r - 1} = \dfrac{u_1(1 - r^n)}{1 - r}, \; r \neq 1$
- Practical problems involving growth or decay, such as questions about interest or depreciation, can be solved using geometric sequences.
  - The formula for compound interest is $FV = PV \times \left(1 + \dfrac{r}{100k}\right)^{kn}$

    where FV = future value, PV = present value, n = number of years, k = number of compounding periods per year, $r\%$ = nominal annual rate of interest.

⚠ EXAM TIPS AND COMMON ERRORS

- Questions often contain parts asking you to find a term of a sequence and a sum of a sequence.
- Many questions on sequences and series involve forming and then solving simultaneous equations.
- You may need to use the list feature on your calculator to solve problems involving sequences.
- You only ever need to use the first sum formula for geometric sequences.
- Sometimes it is useful to remember that $d = u_2 - u_1 = u_3 - u_2 = \ldots$ and $r = \dfrac{u_2}{u_1} = \dfrac{u_3}{u_2} = \ldots$
- Always check whether a question is asking for the interest or the total amount.
- Your calculator may have a finance application which can be helpful.

2.1 ARITHMETIC SEQUENCES AND SERIES

WORKED EXAMPLE 2.1

The third term of an arithmetic sequence is 15 and the sixth term is 27.

(a) Find the tenth term.

(b) Find the sum of the first ten terms.

(c) The sum of the first n terms is 5250. Find the value of n.

(a) $u_3 = u_1 + 2d = 15 \cdots (1)$

$u_6 = u_1 + 5d = 27 \cdots (2)$

$(2) - (1) \Rightarrow 3d = 12$, so $d = 4$

$\therefore u_1 = 15 - 2 \times 4 = 7$

Hence $u_{10} = u_1 + 9d = 7 + 9 \times 4 = 43$

> We need to find the first term and the common difference. Write down the given information in the form of simultaneous equations and then solve.

(b) $S_{10} = \dfrac{10}{2}(u_1 + u_{10})$

$= 5(7 + 43)$

$= 250$

> There are two formulae for the sum of an arithmetic sequence. Since we know the first and last terms, we use $S_n = \dfrac{n}{2}(u_1 + u_n)$.

(c) $5250 = \dfrac{n}{2}(2u_1 + (n-1)d)$

$= \dfrac{n}{2}(14 + 4(n-1))$

> We need to find n, which will be the only unknown in the other sum formula. Form an equation and solve it using a GDC.

From GDC, the solutions are $n = 50$ or $n = -52.5$; but n must be a positive integer, so $n = 50$.

Practice questions 2.1

1. The fifth term of an arithmetic sequence is 8 and the eighth term is 17.

(a) Find the twentieth term.

(b) Find the sum of the first twenty terms.

2. The first four terms of an arithmetic sequence are 8, 7.5, 7, 6.5.

(a) Find the tenth term.

(b) Which term is equal to zero?

(c) The sum of the first n terms is equal to 65. Find the value of n.

2.2 GEOMETRIC SEQUENCES AND SERIES

WORKED EXAMPLE 2.2

Consider the geometric sequence 2, 6, 18, …

(a) Write down the common ratio.

(b) Which is the first term whose value exceeds 1000?

(c) Find the sum of the first 10 terms.

(a) $r = 3$

> ⚠ 'Write down' means that little or no calculation should be necessary. You do not need to show your working.

(b) The sequence continues as
…, 54, 162, 486, 1458, …
So the 7th term is the first to exceed 1000.

> Use the rule $u_n = u_1 \times r^{n-1}$ with $u_1 = 2$ and $r = 3$, i.e. $u_n = 2 \times 3^{n-1}$, and the list function on your GDC to extend the sequence. This could also be done using a graph or table.

(c) $S_{10} = \dfrac{2(3^{10} - 1)}{3 - 1} = 59\,048$

> We can use the formula for the sum of a geometric sequence: $S_n = \dfrac{u_1(r^n - 1)}{r - 1}$.

Practice questions 2.2

3. Consider the geometric sequence 5, 10, 20, 40, ...
   (a) Find the tenth term.
   (b) What is the value of the first term to exceed 3000?
   (c) Find the sum of the first twelve terms.

4. The fifth term of a geometric sequence is 128 and the sixth term is 512.
   (a) Find the common ratio and the first term.
   (b) Which term has a value of 32 768?
   (c) How many terms are needed before the sum of all the terms in the sequence exceeds 100 000?

5. The sum of the first six terms of a geometric sequence is 1365 times its first term. Find the common ratio.

2.3 PRACTICAL PROBLEMS

WORKED EXAMPLE 2.3

Rachel invests £400 in a bank account at 5% annual interest compounded monthly.

(a) How much is in the account after two years? Give your answer to two decimal places.

(b) After how many complete months will the account contain £500?

(a) $FV = 400\left(1 + \dfrac{5}{100 \times 12}\right)^{12 \times 2} = 441.9765\ldots$

So there will be £441.98 in the account after 2 years.

> Use the compound interest formula
> $FV = PV \times \left(1 + \dfrac{r}{100k}\right)^{kn}$ with $PV = 400$, $r = 5$, $k = 12$ (for monthly compounding) and $n = 2$.

(b) $500 = 400\left(1 + \dfrac{5}{100 \times 12}\right)^{n}$

From GDC, $n = 53.7$

So the account will contain £500 after 54 complete months.

> We want to find the value of n for which $FV = 500$. (Note that here we take n to mean the number of months, not years.)
> Use the compound interest formula to write down the equation; then solve it using a calculator.

Practice questions 2.3

6. Aram buys a car for €12,000. The value of the car depreciates by 10% each year.

(a) How much will the car be worth after 3 years? Give your answer to the nearest whole number.

(b) After how many complete years will the value of the car fall to 25% of its original value?

7. Jane takes out a loan for ¥3000. The nominal annual interest rate is 20%.

(a) How much does she owe after 5 years if the interest is compounded annually? Give your answer to the nearest whole number.

(b) How much does she owe after 5 years if the interest is compounded quarterly?

8. Quinn invests $100 at the beginning of each year in a bank account that pays a nominal interest rate of 6% per annum. The interest is added at the end of each year. How much does she have in the account at the end of the third year? Give your answer to two decimal places.

Mixed practice 2

1. The third term of an arithmetic sequence is 5 and the seventh term is 11.

(a) If the first term of the sequence is u_1 and the common difference is d, write down two simultaneous equations in u_1 and d which satisfy this information.

(b) Solve the equations to find u_1 and d.

(c) Find the sum of the first 100 terms of the sequence.

2. A rope of length 300 m is cut into several pieces, the lengths of which form an arithmetic sequence. If the shortest piece is 1 m long and the longest piece is 19 m, find the number of pieces.

3. The fourth term of an arithmetic sequence is 17. The sum of the first twenty terms is 990. Find the first term, a, and the common difference, d, of the sequence.

4. A starting salary for a teacher is $25 000 and there is an annual increase of 3%.

(a) How much will the teacher earn in their 10th year?

(b) How much will the teacher earn in total during a 35-year teaching career?

(c) Find the first year in which the teacher earns more than $35 000.

(d) How many years would the teacher have to work in order to earn a total of $1 million?

5. Calculate the sum of the natural numbers from 1 to 100.

Going for the top 2

1. Mr Liu took out a loan for $500. Without any repayments he owed $700 after two years.

(a) If the interest is compounded annually, what is the annual interest rate?

(b) How much would Mr Liu owe after five years if he continues to make no repayments?

2. Brian and Sandra are both eight years old and share the same birthday. Each week they get pocket money. Currently Brian gets £10 and Sandra gets £15. On his birthday, Brian's weekly pocket money increases by 20%. On her birthday, Sandra's weekly pocket money increases by £1.

(a) How old are they when Brian gets more weekly pocket money than Sandra?

(b) How much has each of them earned by their 18th birthdays?

3 DESCRIPTIVE STATISTICS

WHAT YOU NEED TO KNOW

- Grouping a large sample of data into groups (or classes) makes it easier to summarise.

  - The upper and lower class boundaries are the largest and smallest data values that would be included in that group.

  - The mid-interval value is the value that is half-way between the upper and lower class boundaries.

  - If the data are discrete, the upper and lower class boundaries are as shown in the grouped frequency table. For example, a group 12–15 includes the values 12, 13, 14 and 15, and the mid-interval value is 13.5.

  - If the data are continuous but have been rounded, the class boundaries need to be adjusted. For example, if lengths have been rounded to the nearest metre, then 12–15 means that $11.5 \leq \text{length} < 15.5$, and the mid-interval value is 13.5.

- Three measures of central tendency are the mean, median and mode.

  - The mean is the sum of all the data values divided by the total number of items in the data set. The formula for finding the mean is:

    $$\bar{x} = \frac{\sum_{i=1}^{k} f_i x_i}{n}, \text{ where } n = \sum_{i=1}^{k} f_i \text{ is the total frequency, } x_i \text{ is the } i\text{th distinct data value and } f_i \text{ is}$$

    the frequency of that value.

    - To find the mean for grouped data, assume that every item is at the centre of its group; that is, use the mid-interval value of the group for x_i.

  - The median is the middle of a data set whose values have been arranged in order of size. If there are an odd number of items, the middle is the $\left(\frac{n+1}{2}\right)$th value. If there are an even

    number of items, find the mean of the two middle values, the $\left(\frac{n}{2}\right)$th and $\left(\frac{n}{2}+1\right)$th values.

  - The mode is the most common data value. If the data is grouped, the group with the largest frequency is called the modal group or modal class.

- There are three ways of measuring how spread out a data set is: range, interquartile range and standard deviation.

  - The range is the difference between the highest value and the lowest value.

  - The interquartile range (IQR) is the difference between the upper quartile (Q_3) and the lower quartile (Q_1): $\text{IQR} = Q_3 - Q_1$.

    - To find the quartiles, first divide the data set (with numbers arranged in order) into two halves. The lower quartile is the middle value of the bottom half. The upper quartile is the middle value of the top half.

- The standard deviation is a measure of the average distance of the data values from the mean. It can be calculated using a GDC.

- In a histogram, the height of each bar indicates the frequency of that group. The horizontal scale should be continuous, with each bar covering the group it represents.

- Cumulative frequency is the total frequency up to a certain data value.

  - To draw a cumulative frequency curve from a grouped frequency table, mark the values of the upper class boundaries along the x-axis and plot the cumulative frequency values along the y-axis. Join up the points with a smooth increasing curve.

  - The cumulative frequency curve can be used to find the median and quartiles. For the median, the value on the y-axis will be at $\dfrac{\text{total frequency}}{2}$; for the lower quartile, the value will be at $\dfrac{\text{total frequency}}{4}$, and for the upper quartile it will be at $\dfrac{3 \times \text{total frequency}}{4}$.

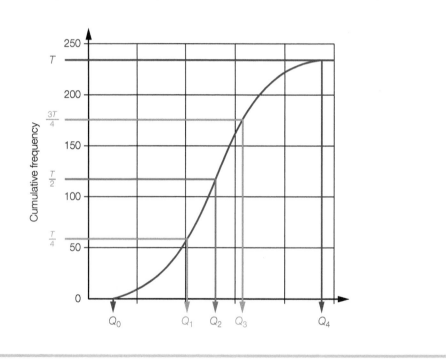

- A box and whisker diagram summarises five important values from a set of data: the smallest value (Q_0), the lower quartile (Q_1), the median (Q_2), the upper quartile (Q_3) and the largest value (Q_4).

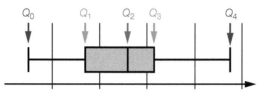

- Each 'whisker' and each half of the 'box' contains a quarter (25%) of all the data.

- Box and whisker diagrams can be used to compare two or more sets of data.

- To compare two sets of data, use the mean and median to compare 'averages', and use the standard deviation and IQR to compare the spread of the data. The data set with the smaller spread can be described as 'less varied' or 'more consistent'.

⚠ EXAM TIPS AND COMMON ERRORS

- When using a calculator to find statistics, make sure you show the numbers that you are using.

- A common error when drawing a cumulative frequency curve is forgetting to plot the first point, which corresponds to zero frequency at the lower boundary of the first group.

- In a box and whisker diagram, the width of the box represents the interquartile range, **not** the number of data values in that range; it is a common mistake to say that a wider box 'contains more people'. When comparing two box and whisker diagrams, always make it clear whether it is the width of the box or its position that is being referred to. 'Higher IQR' should mean that the box is wider, not that the quartiles are larger.

3.1 MEDIAN AND QUARTILES

WORKED EXAMPLE 3.1

Consider the following set of data:

14, 12, 18, 20, 17, 18, 12, 16, 15, x

(a) Given that the median of the data set is 16, find the value of x.

(b) Find the interquartile range of the data.

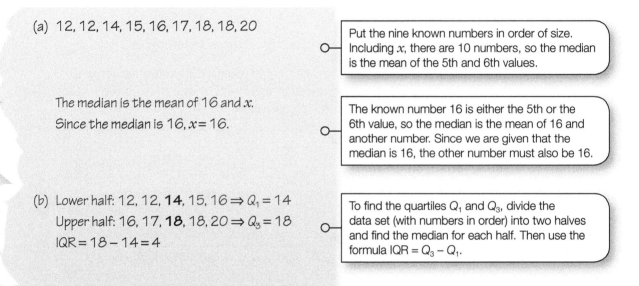

(a) 12, 12, 14, 15, 16, 17, 18, 18, 20

> Put the nine known numbers in order of size. Including x, there are 10 numbers, so the median is the mean of the 5th and 6th values.

The median is the mean of 16 and x.
Since the median is 16, $x = 16$.

> The known number 16 is either the 5th or the 6th value, so the median is the mean of 16 and another number. Since we are given that the median is 16, the other number must also be 16.

(b) Lower half: 12, 12, **14**, 15, 16 $\Rightarrow Q_1 = 14$
Upper half: 16, 17, **18**, 18, 20 $\Rightarrow Q_3 = 18$
IQR $= 18 - 14 = 4$

> To find the quartiles Q_1 and Q_3, divide the data set (with numbers in order) into two halves and find the median for each half. Then use the formula IQR $= Q_3 - Q_1$.

Practice questions 3.1

1. The following data set contains 13 numbers:
2, 4, 5, 10, 12, 14, 14, 16, 18, 21, 23, 23, 25
(a) Explain why the lower quartile is 7.5.
(b) Find the interquartile range of the data.

2. The median of the numbers $x - 2, x + 1, x + 3, x + 6, x + 7, x + 10$ is 6.5.
Find the value of x.

3. Find the median and the interquartile range of the grades summarised in the table:

Grade	2	3	4	5	6	7
Frequency	5	12	36	42	27	19

When entering frequency table data into your GDC, check that the value of n is what you expect – in this case 141.

3.2 MEAN, STANDARD DEVIATION AND FREQUENCY HISTOGRAMS

WORKED EXAMPLE 3.2

The histogram below shows the masses of some dogs.

(a) How many dogs were included in the sample?

(b) What is the modal group?

(c) Estimate the standard deviation of the masses.

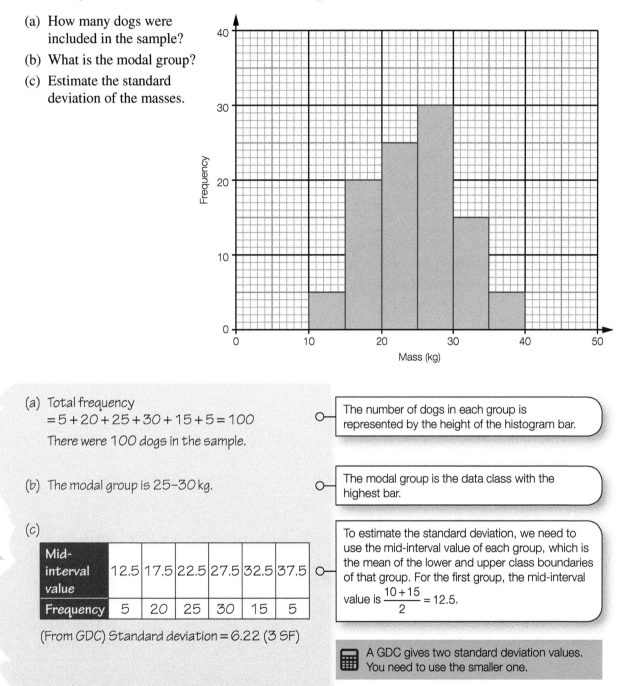

(a) Total frequency
$$= 5 + 20 + 25 + 30 + 15 + 5 = 100$$
There were 100 dogs in the sample.

> The number of dogs in each group is represented by the height of the histogram bar.

(b) The modal group is 25–30 kg.

> The modal group is the data class with the highest bar.

(c)

Mid-interval value	12.5	17.5	22.5	27.5	32.5	37.5
Frequency	5	20	25	30	15	5

(From GDC) Standard deviation = 6.22 (3 SF)

> To estimate the standard deviation, we need to use the mid-interval value of each group, which is the mean of the lower and upper class boundaries of that group. For the first group, the mid-interval value is $\dfrac{10+15}{2} = 12.5$.

> A GDC gives two standard deviation values. You need to use the smaller one.

Practice questions 3.2

4. The mean of the numbers 4, 5, 3, 3, 5 and k is 3.5.
   (a) Find the value of k.
   (b) Find the standard deviation of the numbers.

5. The frequency table shows the heights of 26 trees. The mean height is 6.5 m.

Height (m)	3	5	y	10
Frequency	4	x	11	5

   (a) Find the values of x and y.
   (b) Calculate the standard deviation of the heights.

6. The heights of 50 buildings, rounded to the nearest metre, are summarised in the following table:

Height (m)	12–17	18–23	24–29	30–35
Frequency	12	14	16	8

   (a) Write down the upper and lower boundaries of the 24–29 class.
   (b) Draw a histogram to represent the data.
   (c) Find the mean and standard deviation of the heights.

7. The ages of 35 teachers are recorded in the table:

Age (years)	21–30	31–40	41–50	51–60	61–70
Frequency	5	9	11	7	3

   (a) Write down the upper and lower boundaries of the 21–30 group and find its mid-interval value.
   (b) Draw a histogram to represent the data.
   (c) Find the mean and standard deviation of the ages.

8. The times taken by a group of athletes to run 100 m were recorded in the table and histogram.

Time, t, in seconds	Frequency
$10.0 < t \leq 10.5$	8
$< t \leq$	11
$11.0 < t \leq 11.5$	
$11.5 < t \leq 12.0$	16

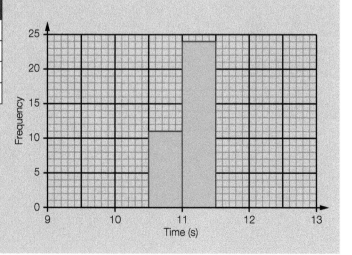

   (a) How many athletes took part?
   (b) Use the table to complete the histogram.
   (c) Use the histogram to complete the table.

3.3 CUMULATIVE FREQUENCY

WORKED EXAMPLE 3.3

The cumulative frequency curve below represents the heights of 36 children.

Estimate the median and the interquartile range of the heights.

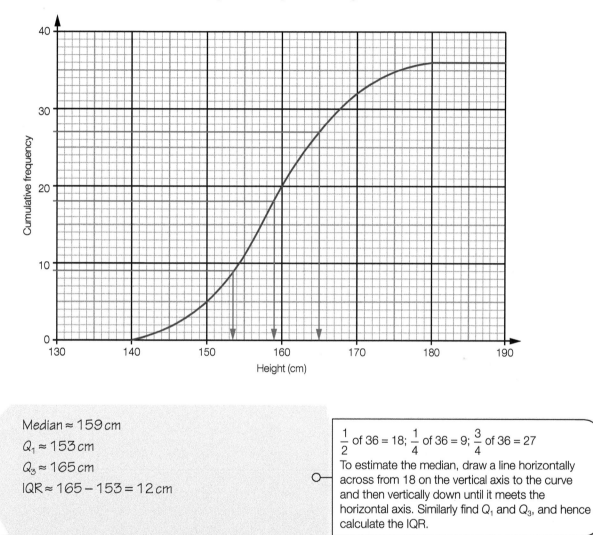

Median ≈ 159 cm

$Q_1 \approx 153$ cm

$Q_3 \approx 165$ cm

IQR ≈ 165 − 153 = 12 cm

$\dfrac{1}{2}$ of 36 = 18; $\dfrac{1}{4}$ of 36 = 9; $\dfrac{3}{4}$ of 36 = 27

To estimate the median, draw a line horizontally across from 18 on the vertical axis to the curve and then vertically down until it meets the horizontal axis. Similarly find Q_1 and Q_3, and hence calculate the IQR.

Practice questions 3.3

9. The ages of students at a school are summarised in the table.

(a) Draw a cumulative frequency curve to represent the information.

(b) Find the median age.

(c) The oldest 10% of the students are older than m years. Find the value of m.

Age (years)	Frequency
4–7	20
8–11	40
12–15	80
16–19	60

10. Use the cumulative frequency curve to complete the frequency table.

Height, h (cm)	Frequency
$150 \le h < 160$	8
$160 \le h < 168$	
$168 \le h < 175$	
$175 \le h < 190$	

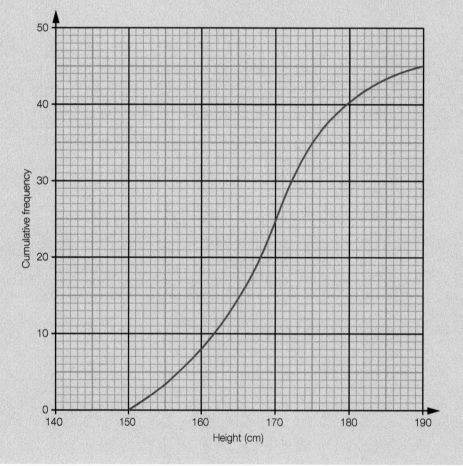

3.4 BOX AND WHISKER DIAGRAMS AND COMPARING DATA SETS

WORKED EXAMPLE 3.4

The English test marks (in %) of a group of students are summarised in the following diagram.

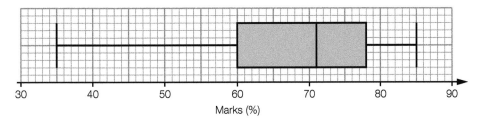

Marks (%)

The marks for the same group of students on a Mathematics test had the following features:

lowest mark 24%, highest mark 93%, lower quartile 43%, median 62%, upper quartile 72%.

(a) Draw a box and whisker diagram for the Mathematics marks.
(b) Compare the performance of the group in the two tests.

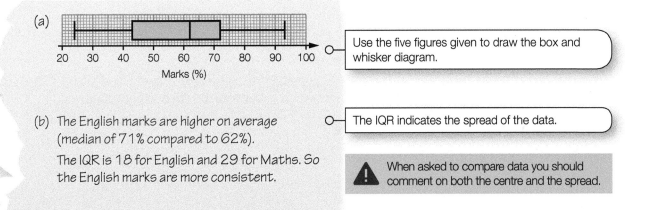

(a)

Marks (%)

Use the five figures given to draw the box and whisker diagram.

(b) The English marks are higher on average (median of 71% compared to 62%).

The IQR is 18 for English and 29 for Maths. So the English marks are more consistent.

The IQR indicates the spread of the data.

⚠ When asked to compare data you should comment on both the centre and the spread.

Practice questions 3.4

11. Draw a box and whisker diagram to represent the following data:

Smallest	Largest	Mean	Standard deviation	Median	Q_1	Q_3
12	45	31.6	5.5	35	23	42

12. Two schools took part in a cross-country race. The times are summarised in the diagram below. Write three comments comparing the times of the students from the two schools.

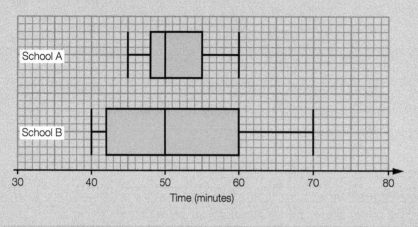

When comparing two sets of data, always refer to the context of the question. For example, instead of 'the men have a higher mean' you should say 'the men are older on average'.

Mixed practice 3

1. The mode of the following list of numbers is 5:

1, 2, 2, 5, 4, 5, 6, 3, 6, x.

(a) Find the value of x.

(b) Find the median of the numbers.

2. The results of a Physics exam for two different schools are summarised in the table below:

	Lowest mark	Highest mark	Median	Lower quartile	Upper quartile
School 1	20	52	32	26	41
School 2	31	60	39	34	48

(a) Calculate the interquartile ranges of the marks for the two schools.

(b) Draw two box and whisker diagrams to represent the results.

(c) Describe one similarity and one difference between the two schools' results.

3. The table shows the History grades of IB students at a college:

Grade	3	4	5	6	7
Number of students	4	12	x	17	9

(a) Given that the mean grade is 5.23 (to three significant figures), find the value of x.

(b) Find the median grade.

4. The maximum speed (in km/h) for 130 cars is recorded in the frequency table:

Speed (km/h)	140–160	160–175	175–185	185–190	190–200
Number of cars	14	35	41	23	17

(a) Draw a cumulative frequency curve to represent the information.

(b) Draw a box and whisker diagram to represent the data.

(c) Find the interquartile range of the speeds.

5. The ages of employees at a company are summarised in the cumulative frequency table. The youngest employee is 16 years old.

(a) Draw a histogram to represent the data.

(b) Estimate the mean and standard deviation of the ages.

Age (years)	Cumulative frequency
≤ 26	12
≤ 36	46
≤ 46	82
≤ 56	90

6. All athletes in a club competed in a long jump competition. Their results are shown in the histogram:

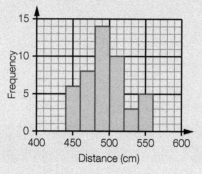

(a) Use the histogram to complete the frequency table, where the distances have been rounded to the nearest centimetre.

Distance (cm)	441–460	461–480	481–500	501–520	521–540	541–560
Frequency						

(b) Estimate the mean and the standard deviation of the distances.

(c) Draw a cumulative frequency curve to represent the information.

(d) (i) Find the percentage of athletes who jumped further than 4.80 m.

   (ii) Two athletes are selected at random. What is the probability that they both jumped further than 4.80 m?

(e) The top 20% of athletes will qualify for a regional competition. Estimate the minimum distance required for qualification.

Going for the top 3

1. The frequency table summarises 36 pieces of
   data with mean $\dfrac{47}{9}$. Find the values of x and y.

Value	4	5	6	7
Frequency	9	13	x	y

2. The set of numbers 3, 2, 3, 7, 10, 5, 7, 12, x, y, z has mode 3, median 6 and mean 6. Find the
   values of x, y and z.

3. The histogram shows the times a group of 55 students
   took to complete their homework.

   (a) Estimate the number of students who took:

       (i) more than 25 minutes

       (ii) more than 37 minutes.

   (b) Given that a student took more than 25 minutes to
   complete their homework, find the probability that
   they took more than 37 minutes.

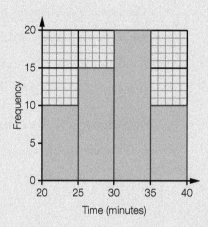

4 SET THEORY AND VENN DIAGRAMS

WHAT YOU NEED TO KNOW

- A set is a list of objects with a name; for example, $A = \{$Apples, Pears, Bananas$\}$ where 'Pears' is an element of that set.

  - The number of elements in A is denoted by $n(A)$.

  - $x \in A$ means that x is an element of A.

  - $x \notin A$ means that x is not an element of A.

  - A set which contains no elements is called an empty set, denoted by $\varnothing$.

- A Venn diagram is a way of representing sets by areas.

  - U is the universal set, containing all relevant objects.

  - $A \cup B$, 'A union B', is the list of all elements in either set without repeats.

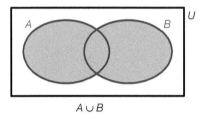

$A \cup B$

  - $A \cap B$, 'A intersection B', is the list of all elements in the overlap of both sets.

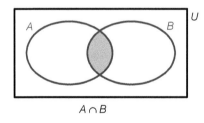

$A \cap B$

- A', the complement of A, contains everything that is not in A.

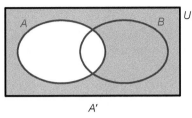

A'

- $A \subset B$ means that A is a proper subset of B, i.e. every element of set A is contained in set B. $A \subseteq B$ means that A is either a proper subset of B or the same set as B.

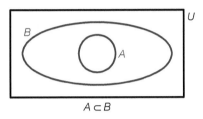

$A \subset B$

⚠ EXAM TIPS AND COMMON ERRORS

- When completing a Venn diagram, start in the middle and work outwards. Make sure that you label each area with the number of objects in just that area.

- If you are asked to draw a Venn diagram to represent a situation, do not assume that all the circles overlap.

4.1 SET NOTATION

WORKED EXAMPLE 4.1

The universal set U is the set of positive whole numbers less than 15. A and B are subsets of U such that A is the set of multiples of 3 and B is the set of prime numbers.

List the elements of the following sets:

(a) A 　　　　　 (b) $A \cap B$ 　　　　　 (c) $A \cup B'$

(a) $\{3, 6, 9, 12\}$

(b) $\{3\}$

> $A \cap B$ means everything that is in the overlap of the sets A and B, where:
> $A = \{\mathbf{3}, 6, 9, 12\}$
> $B = \{2, \mathbf{3}, 5, 7, 11, 13\}$

(c) $\{1, 3, 4, 6, 8, 9, 10, 12, 14\}$

> $A \cup B'$ means everything in U that is in A or not in B, so combine $A = \{3, 6, 9, 12\}$ with $B' = \{1, 4, 6, 8, 9, 10, 12, 14\}$.

Practice questions 4.1

1. The universal set U is the set of positive whole numbers less than or equal to 10. A and B are subsets of U such that A is the set of factors of 20 and B is the set of even numbers. List the elements of the following sets:
   (a) A 　　　　　 (b) $A \cap B$ 　　　　　 (c) $A' \cup B'$

2. In the universal set of positive whole numbers, A is the set of multiples of 4 and B is the set of multiples of 8. Which of the following statements are true?
   (a) $A \subset B$ 　　 (b) $A \cup B = B$ 　　 (c) $B \cap A' = \varnothing$ 　　 (d) $7 \in B'$

3. Which of these statements are always true for all sets A and B?
   (a) $A \cap A = A$ 　 (b) $A \cup A' = U$ 　　 (c) $\varnothing \subset A$ 　　 (d) $(A \cup B) \subset B$

4.2 VENN DIAGRAMS WITH SHADING

WORKED EXAMPLE 4.2

Shade the region represented by $(A \cup B) \cap C'$ in this Venn diagram.

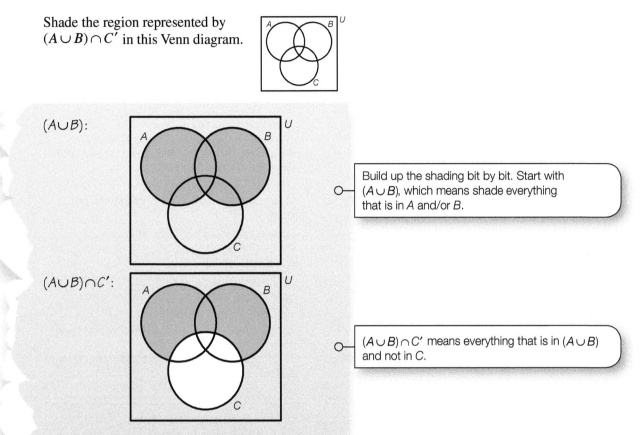

$(A \cup B)$:

Build up the shading bit by bit. Start with $(A \cup B)$, which means shade everything that is in A and/or B.

$(A \cup B) \cap C'$:

$(A \cup B) \cap C'$ means everything that is in $(A \cup B)$ and not in C.

Practice questions 4.2

4. In the Venn diagram on the right, shade the region represented by $A' \cap B' \cap C'$.

5. In the Venn diagram on the right, shade the region represented by $(A \cup B)' \cup C$.

6. Use set notation to describe the shaded region in this Venn diagram.

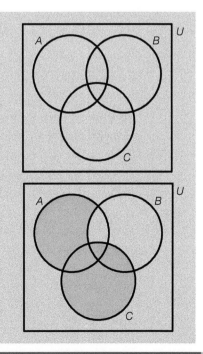

4.3 APPLICATIONS OF SET THEORY AND VENN DIAGRAMS

WORKED EXAMPLE 4.3

A class has 25 students. 16 of them play basketball, 12 of them play football and 12 swim. 8 play both basketball and football. 9 play football and swim. 7 play basketball and swim. 5 students play all three sports. How many students play none of the sports?

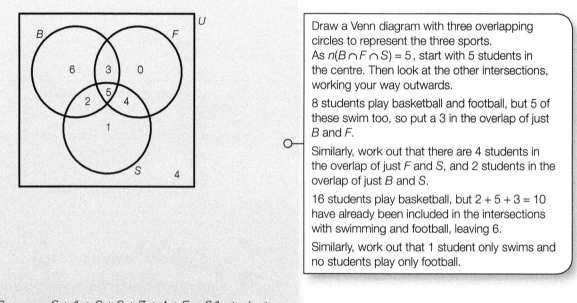

Draw a Venn diagram with three overlapping circles to represent the three sports. As $n(B \cap F \cap S) = 5$, start with 5 students in the centre. Then look at the other intersections, working your way outwards.

8 students play basketball and football, but 5 of these swim too, so put a 3 in the overlap of just B and F.

Similarly, work out that there are 4 students in the overlap of just F and S, and 2 students in the overlap of just B and S.

16 students play basketball, but $2 + 5 + 3 = 10$ have already been included in the intersections with swimming and football, leaving 6.

Similarly, work out that 1 student only swims and no students play only football.

There are $6 + 1 + 0 + 2 + 3 + 4 + 5 = 21$ students who play basketball, play football or swim.

So there are $25 - 21 = 4$ students who do not play any of these sports.

Use the fact that there are 25 students in total.

Practice questions 4.3

7. Of a group of 70 students, 43 have their own computer and 29 have their own TV. 11 students have both a TV and a computer. How many students have neither a computer nor a TV?

8. In a class of 20 students, 16 study Biology and 17 study Physics. 2 students study neither subject. How many students study both Biology and Physics?

9. In a group of 45 children, 13 have a dog, 21 have a cat and 24 have a fish. 6 have both a dog and a cat, 13 have both a cat and a fish, and 3 have both a dog and a fish. 2 have all three types of pets.
   (a) How many children do not have a dog, cat or fish?
   (b) How many have a dog but not a cat or a fish?

Mixed practice 4

1. In the universal set of positive numbers less than 20, S is the set of perfect square numbers and E is the set of even numbers.

   (a) List the elements in $S \cap E$.

   (b) Find $n(S \cup E')$.

2. In a sample of 40 Mathematical Studies examination papers, 32 contain questions on Venn diagrams and 30 contain questions on currency conversion. 24 contain questions on both Venn diagrams and currency conversions. How many papers contain questions on neither topic?

3. In this diagram shade the area that represents $(A \cap B') \cup C'$.

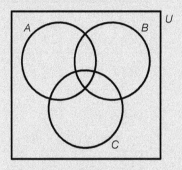

4. In a class of 30 students, 22 study French and 17 study Spanish. 8 students study neither language. How many students study both?

5. If $n(A \cap B) = 0$, draw a Venn diagram showing the two sets A and B. Shade the region $A' \cap B'$.

6. A survey asked students about what they had done over the weekend. 20 did homework, 16 went to the gym and 15 went to the cinema. 4 did homework and went to the gym, 3 went to the gym and the cinema, and 5 went to the cinema and did homework. No students did all three activities, and 3 students did none of these activities.

   (a) How many students were surveyed?

   (b) What percentage of students did homework but did not go to the gym or the cinema?

Going for the top 4

1. (a) How many (non-empty) proper subsets does a set of size 3 have?

   (b) How many (non-empty) proper subsets does a set of size 4 have?

   (c) How many (non-empty) proper subsets does a set of size n have?

2. In a group of 50 students, 38 have read Shakespeare, 33 have read Austen and 28 have read Wilde. 22 have read Shakespeare and Austen, 16 have read Austen and Wilde, and 18 have read Wilde and Shakespeare. 3 students have read none of these authors. How many students have read all three authors?

5 LOGIC

WHAT YOU NEED TO KNOW

- A proposition is a statement that is either true or false.
  The statement 'This car is yellow' is a proposition, but 'Stop!' is not a proposition.

- Propositions can be connected to form compound statements.

Compound statement	Symbolic notation	What it means	When it is true
Negation	$\neg p$	not p	True when p is false
Conjunction	$p \wedge q$	p and q	True when both p and q are true
Disjunction	$p \vee q$	p or q	True when either p or q is true or both p and q are true
Exclusive disjunction	$p \veebar q$	p or q but not both	True when either p or q is true but not both
Implication	$p \Rightarrow q$	if p then q	True unless p is true and q is false
Equivalence	$p \Leftrightarrow q$	p if and only if q	True when both p and q are true or when both p and q are false

 For implication it is important to use the words 'If...then', not 'therefore'.

- A truth table is a list of all possible values for the basic propositions and their compound propositions.

p	q	$\neg p$	$p \wedge q$	$p \vee q$	$p \veebar q$	$p \Rightarrow q$	$p \Leftrightarrow q$
T	T	F	T	T	F	T	T
T	F	F	F	T	T	F	F
F	T	T	F	T	T	T	F
F	F	T	F	F	F	T	T

⚠ Questions involving three propositions may be set with some of the columns in the truth table filled in. Use the short truth table in the Formula booklet to help you complete them.

- Logical equivalence, tautology and contradiction are all tested using truth tables.
  - Two compound statements are logically equivalent when the final columns of their truth tables are exactly the same.
  - A logical tautology is always true, even if the initial propositions are false. All the entries in the final column of the truth table are T.
  - A logical contradiction is never true. All the entries in the final column of the truth table are F.
  - If a logical implication is a tautology, then it represents a valid argument.
  - When an argument is not a tautology, it may still be valid in a certain context if, in that context, the conclusion always follows.

- If $p \Rightarrow q$, then:
  - $q \Rightarrow p$ is the converse
  - $\neg p \Rightarrow \neg q$ is the inverse
  - $\neg q \Rightarrow \neg p$ is the contrapositive.
    - If the original implication is true, the converse or inverse are not necessarily true, but the contrapositive is true.

5.1 CONSTRUCTING TRUTH TABLES

WORKED EXAMPLE 5.1

Construct a truth table for $p \vee (q \wedge r)$.

 Be systematic in how you lay out the truth table.

p	q	r	$q \wedge r$	$p \vee (q \wedge r)$
T	T	T	T	T
T	T	F	F	T
T	F	T	F	T
T	F	F	F	T
F	T	T	T	T
F	T	F	F	F
F	F	T	F	F
F	F	F	F	F

Start with three columns for the initial propositions, p, q and r, and build the argument stage by stage: add a column for $q \wedge r$ and then a final column for the whole statement.

Work down each column row by row. For example:

In the second row, p is true, q is true and r is false; so $q \wedge r$ is false (since not both q and r are true), and hence $p \vee (q \wedge r)$ is true as at least one of p or $q \wedge r$ is true.

In the sixth row, $p \vee (q \wedge r)$ is false because neither p nor $q \wedge r$ is true.

Practice questions 5.1

1. Complete the truth table below.

p	q	r	$q \vee r$	$p \wedge (q \vee r)$
T	T	T	T	T
T	T	F		
T	F	T		
T	F	F		
F	T	T		
F	T	F		
F	F	T		
F	F	F		

5.2 LOGICAL EQUIVALENCE, TAUTOLOGY AND CONTRADICTION

WORKED EXAMPLE 5.2

Show that $\neg p \wedge \neg q$ is logically equivalent to $\neg(p \vee q)$.

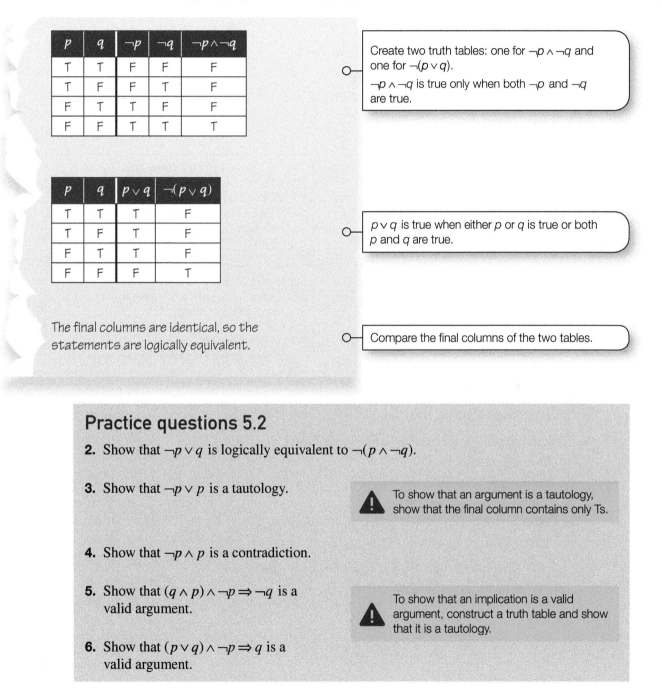

p	q	$\neg p$	$\neg q$	$\neg p \wedge \neg q$
T	T	F	F	F
T	F	F	T	F
F	T	T	F	F
F	F	T	T	T

Create two truth tables: one for $\neg p \wedge \neg q$ and one for $\neg(p \vee q)$.

$\neg p \wedge \neg q$ is true only when both $\neg p$ and $\neg q$ are true.

p	q	$p \vee q$	$\neg(p \vee q)$
T	T	T	F
T	F	T	F
F	T	T	F
F	F	F	T

$p \vee q$ is true when either p or q is true or both p and q are true.

The final columns are identical, so the statements are logically equivalent.

Compare the final columns of the two tables.

Practice questions 5.2

2. Show that $\neg p \vee q$ is logically equivalent to $\neg(p \wedge \neg q)$.

3. Show that $\neg p \vee p$ is a tautology.

> ⚠ To show that an argument is a tautology, show that the final column contains only Ts.

4. Show that $\neg p \wedge p$ is a contradiction.

5. Show that $(q \wedge p) \wedge \neg p \Rightarrow \neg q$ is a valid argument.

> ⚠ To show that an implication is a valid argument, construct a truth table and show that it is a tautology.

6. Show that $(p \vee q) \wedge \neg p \Rightarrow q$ is a valid argument.

5.3 COMPOUND STATEMENTS

WORKED EXAMPLE 5.3

The propositions p, q and r are defined as follows:

p: I am wearing glasses. $\qquad$ q: I am reading. $\qquad$ r: I am driving.

(a) Write symbolic statements for the following sentences:
   (i) I am reading and I am wearing glasses.
   (ii) If I am reading then I am not wearing glasses.
(b) Write in words the symbolic statement $(p \wedge \neg q) \Rightarrow r$.

(a) (i) $p \wedge q$

> The 'and' in the compound statement means that this is a conjunction.

   (ii) $q \Rightarrow \neg p$

> The 'If' in the compound statement means it is an implication, and 'I am not wearing glasses' is the negation of p.

(b) If I am wearing glasses and not reading then I am driving.

> The $\Rightarrow$ indicates 'If ... then'.
> p is 'I am wearing glasses'; $\wedge$ means 'and'; and $\neg q$ is 'I am not reading'.
> Put it all together, with 'If' coming at the start of the statement.

Practice questions 5.3

7. The propositions p, q and r are defined as follows:
   p: There are puddles.
   q: It is raining.
   r: I am wearing a raincoat.
   (a) Write the following statements using symbolic notation:
      (i) There are puddles but it is not raining.
      (ii) The fact that it is raining is implied by the puddles.
   (b) Write in words the symbolic statement $(p \vee q) \Leftrightarrow r$.

5.4 CONVERSE, INVERSE AND CONTRAPOSITIVE

WORKED EXAMPLE 5.4

Let p represent the proposition:

'If I revise I will pass the Studies examination.'

(a) State the inverse of p.
(b) State the contrapositive of p.
(c) If p is true, which of the inverse or the contrapositive is also necessarily true?

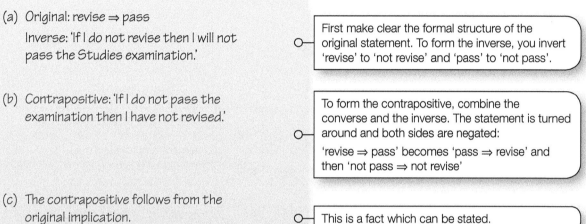

(a) Original: revise ⇒ pass

Inverse: 'If I do not revise then I will not pass the Studies examination.'

First make clear the formal structure of the original statement. To form the inverse, you invert 'revise' to 'not revise' and 'pass' to 'not pass'.

(b) Contrapositive: 'If I do not pass the examination then I have not revised.'

To form the contrapositive, combine the converse and the inverse. The statement is turned around and both sides are negated:

'revise ⇒ pass' becomes 'pass ⇒ revise' and then 'not pass ⇒ not revise'

(c) The contrapositive follows from the original implication.

This is a fact which can be stated.

Practice questions 5.4

8. Let p represent the proposition: 'Smiling implies that you are happy.'
For this statement, write in words:

    (a) the converse of p (b) the inverse of p (c) the contrapositive of p.

9. Let p represent the proposition: 'If nobody gets vaccinated then there will be an epidemic.'
Which of these statements is the contrapositive of p?

A: 'If there was not an epidemic then somebody got vaccinated.'

B: 'If everybody gets vaccinated then there will not be an epidemic.'

C: 'If there was not an epidemic then everybody got vaccinated.'

D: 'If somebody gets vaccinated then there will not be an epidemic.'

5.5 CHECKING VALIDITY OF ARGUMENTS WITHOUT TRUTH TABLES

WORKED EXAMPLE 5.5

The propositions p, q and r are defined as follows:

p: x is a multiple of 3.
q: x is a multiple of 5.
r: x is a multiple of 15.

Decide which of the following arguments are valid, giving your reasons:

(a) $p \Rightarrow r$

(b) $p \wedge q \Rightarrow r$

(c) $q \Rightarrow \neg p$

(a) This statement means that 'if x is a multiple of 3, then it is a multiple of 15'. However, 9 is an example which shows that this is not always true, so this argument is not valid.

> First, write the symbolic statement in words. Then look for an example which demonstrates that the statement is not always true.

(b) This statement means that 'if x is a multiple of 3 and a multiple of 5, then it is a multiple of 15'. This argument is valid.

(c) This statement means that 'if x is a multiple of 5, then it is not a multiple of 3'. However, 15 is an example which shows that this is not always true, so this argument is not valid.

Practice questions 5.5

10. The propositions p, q and r are defined as follows:

p: $x \in \mathbb{R}$ q: $x \in \mathbb{Q}$ r: $x \in \mathbb{N}$

Decide which of the following arguments are valid, giving your reasons:

(a) $r \Rightarrow p$ (b) $p \wedge q \Rightarrow p$ (c) $p \wedge \neg q \Rightarrow r$

Mixed practice 5

1. Consider the following two propositions, relating to a whole number:

   p: The number ends in 2.

   q: The number is even.

   (a) Write in words the following symbolic statements:

       (i) $p \vee q$ (ii) $p \Rightarrow q$ (iii)   The inverse of $p \Rightarrow q$.

   (b) Write the following using symbolic notation:

       (i)   The converse of $p \Rightarrow q$ (ii)   The contrapositive of $p \Rightarrow q$.

2. (a) Construct truth tables for the following statements:

       (i) $(p \wedge q) \wedge \neg p$ (ii) $\neg p \vee q$

       (iii) $(p \vee \neg p) \vee q$ (iv) $p \Rightarrow q$

   (b) (i)   Which of the statements in part (a) is a contradiction?

       (ii)   Which of the statements in part (a) is a tautology?

       (iii) Which two of the statements in part (a) are logically equivalent?

3. The two propositions p and q are defined as follows:

   p: John is studying mathematics.

   q: Iqbal is studying mathematics.

   (a) Write the following statements in symbols:

       (i)   Neither John nor Iqbal studies mathematics.

       (ii)   It is not the case that John and Iqbal both study mathematics.

       (iii) John studies mathematics if and only if Iqbal studies mathematics.

   (b) Write in words $p \veebar q$.

4. (a) Construct a truth table for $(p \Rightarrow q) \wedge (q \Rightarrow r)$.

   (b) Hence show that $(p \Rightarrow q) \wedge (q \Rightarrow r)$ is not logically equivalent to $p \Rightarrow r$.

5. (a) Construct a truth table for $(p \vee q) \wedge (\neg p \wedge \neg q)$.

   (b) Which of the following words could be used to describe $(p \vee q) \wedge (\neg p \wedge \neg q)$?

       converse, contrapositive, contradiction, inverse, tautology

6. (a) Write down the truth table for $p \Rightarrow q$.

   (b) Hence determine whether the argument $\big((p \Rightarrow q) \wedge (p \Rightarrow \neg q)\big) \Rightarrow \neg p$ is valid.

7. Let p and q be the statements:

p: The object is a square.

q: The object is a rectangle.

(a) Consider the following logic statement: 'If the object is not a rectangle, then it is not a square.'

    (i) Write the statement in symbolic form.

    (ii) Write down in words the contrapositive of the statement.

(b) Use a truth table to show that $p \wedge q \Rightarrow p$ is a valid argument.

(c) State with reasons which one of the following statements is valid in this context:

$p \Rightarrow q$

$q \Rightarrow p$

Going for the top 5

1. Write down the inverse, converse and contrapositive of $p \Rightarrow \neg q$.

2. (a) Show that $\neg p \vee q$ is logically equivalent to $p \Rightarrow q$.

(b) Find a statement involving conjunctions and disjunctions of p and q which is logically equivalent to $p \Leftrightarrow q$.

3. (a) Show that $(p \Rightarrow q) \Rightarrow (\neg q \Rightarrow \neg p)$ is a valid argument.

(b) Interpret what this means in terms of the converse, inverse or contrapositive.

4. Show that disjunction is distributive over conjunction.

6 PROBABILITY

- All probabilities lie between 0 and 1.

- The general formula for calculating the probability of an event A is:

$$P(A) = \frac{\text{number of outcomes in } A}{\text{total number of outcomes}}$$

- The complement of an event A, denoted by A', consists of all the possibilities that are not in A:

$$P(A') = 1 - P(A)$$

- The expected number of times an event will occur in n attempts is equal to $P(A) \times n$.

- The probability of an event can be found by listing or counting all possible outcomes. The probabilities of combined events are often best found using sample space diagrams, two-way tables, Venn diagrams or tree diagrams.

  - For combined events, the probability of A or B occurring (the union of A and B) can be found using the formula:

    $$P(A \cup B) = P(A) + P(B) - P(A \cap B)$$

    where $P(A \cap B)$ is the probability of events A and B both occurring.

  - Mutually exclusive events are events which cannot happen at the same time:

    - $P(A \cap B) = 0$
    - $P(A \cup B) = P(A) + P(B)$

- The probability of event A happening given that event B has already happened is known as conditional probability and is denoted by $P(A \mid B)$, which means 'the probability of A given B':

$$P(A \mid B) = \frac{P(A \cap B)}{P(B)}$$

- Independent events are events which do not affect each other.
  If two events are independent:

$$P(A \cap B) = P(A)\,P(B)$$

  - To show that two events are independent, you must show that this formula holds.

- Exam questions will always be set in context, so you will never *need* to use formulae. Try to use your understanding of the probability rather than just the formulae in the Formula booklet.

- All probabilities lie between 0 and 1. Try to estimate the answer before you do the calculation to make sure the answer is sensible.

- When interpreting probability questions, pay particular attention to whether the required probability is conditional or not.

6.1 BASIC PROBABILITY

WORKED EXAMPLE 6.1

A bag contains 12 green marbles, 8 red marbles and 10 blue marbles.

(a) If one marble is taken from the bag, find the probability that it is red.

(b) If two marbles are taken from the bag without replacement, what is the probability that they are both red?

(c) If one marble is taken and it is not blue, find the probability that it is red.

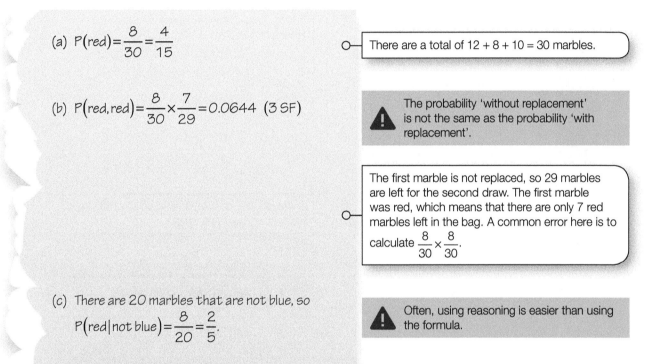

(a) $P(\text{red}) = \dfrac{8}{30} = \dfrac{4}{15}$

There are a total of $12 + 8 + 10 = 30$ marbles.

(b) $P(\text{red, red}) = \dfrac{8}{30} \times \dfrac{7}{29} = 0.0644$ (3 SF)

⚠ The probability 'without replacement' is not the same as the probability 'with replacement'.

The first marble is not replaced, so 29 marbles are left for the second draw. The first marble was red, which means that there are only 7 red marbles left in the bag. A common error here is to calculate $\dfrac{8}{30} \times \dfrac{8}{30}$.

(c) There are 20 marbles that are not blue, so
$P(\text{red} \mid \text{not blue}) = \dfrac{8}{20} = \dfrac{2}{5}$.

⚠ Often, using reasoning is easier than using the formula.

Practice questions 6.1

1. Two letters are chosen at random without replacement from the word 'MATHEMATICS'. Find the probability that:
  (a) the first letter is a T   (b) both letters are M
  (c) the first letter is an I given that it is a vowel.

2. A class consists of 13 boys and 12 girls. Two children are selected at random. Find the probability that:
  (a) they are both boys   (b) they are of different genders.

6.2 SAMPLE SPACE DIAGRAMS AND CALCULATING PROBABILITY

WORKED EXAMPLE 6.2

Two dice are rolled. The higher number showing is recorded.

(a) Draw a sample space diagram to show all the possible outcomes.
(b) What is the probability that the number recorded is a 6?
(c) What is the probability that the number recorded is a 6 given that it is a 5 or a 6?

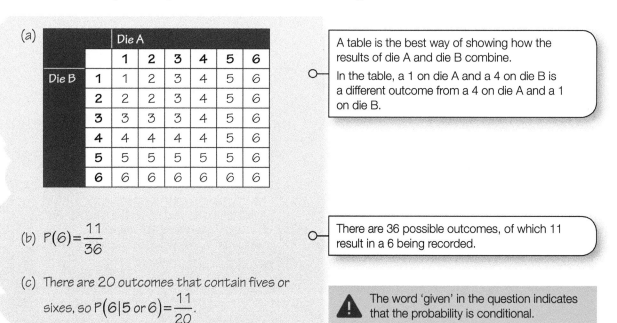

(a)

	Die A					
Die B	**1**	**2**	**3**	**4**	**5**	**6**
1	1	2	3	4	5	6
2	2	2	3	4	5	6
3	3	3	3	4	5	6
4	4	4	4	4	5	6
5	5	5	5	5	5	6
6	6	6	6	6	6	6

A table is the best way of showing how the results of die A and die B combine.

In the table, a 1 on die A and a 4 on die B is a different outcome from a 4 on die A and a 1 on die B.

(b) $P(6) = \dfrac{11}{36}$

There are 36 possible outcomes, of which 11 result in a 6 being recorded.

(c) There are 20 outcomes that contain fives or sixes, so $P(6 | 5 \text{ or } 6) = \dfrac{11}{20}$.

⚠ The word 'given' in the question indicates that the probability is conditional.

Practice questions 6.2

3. A die is rolled twice and the results of the two rolls are summed.
  (a) Draw a sample space diagram to show all the possible outcomes.
  (b) What is the probability that the sum is 3?
  (c) What is the most likely sum?
  (d) If the sum is greater than 8, find the probability that it is 12.

4. A red spinner has sectors labelled 1, 1, 1, 4, 5, 6. A blue spinner has sectors labelled 1, 2, 3, 4, 5, 6. The two spinners are spun and the scores are added together. Find the probability that:
  (a) the total is greater than 7   (b) the total is 10 given that it is not 7.

6.3 INTERPRETING TABLES

WORKED EXAMPLE 6.3

The following table shows the eye colour and hair colour of 100 children in a school.

		Hair colour			
		Fair	Red	Brown	Black
Eyes	Blue	24	4	15	0
	Brown	4	1	20	32

If one of the children is chosen at random, find the probability that the child has:

(a) blue eyes   (b) blue eyes and fair hair   (c) blue eyes given that the child is fair.

(a) $P(\text{blue eyes}) = \dfrac{43}{100}$

○— The total of the 'Blue' row is $24 + 4 + 15 + 0 = 43$.

(b) $P(\text{blue eyes and fair}) = \dfrac{24}{100} = \dfrac{6}{25}$

○— Read the answer directly from the table.

(c) $P(\text{blue eyes}\,|\,\text{fair}) = \dfrac{24}{28} = \dfrac{6}{7}$

○— There are $24 + 4 = 28$ fair pupils.

⚠ Make sure you do not confuse the situations in parts (b) and (c).

Practice questions 6.3

5. A shop sells cod and haddock in three different sizes. The table shows the numbers of each sold in one week.

(a) How many fish were sold in this week?

(b) Use the sales figures for this week to estimate the probability that a randomly sold fish is a:

     (i) large cod   (ii) haddock   (iii) haddock given that it is not large.

		Size		
		Small	Medium	Large
Fish	Cod	18	26	22
	Haddock	14	18	17

6. Students studying the IB in a school select a humanities and a maths subject. The table shows the number of students studying each combination.

Find the probability that a randomly chosen student selects:

(a) Maths Studies and Economics

(b) Maths Studies or Economics

(c) Maths Studies given that they select Economics.

		Humanities		
		History	Geography	Economics
Maths	Studies	32	18	6
	Standard	12	15	12
	Higher	8	9	12

6.4 TREE DIAGRAMS

WORKED EXAMPLE 6.4

One quarter of the time Mbeki takes the bus to school. Otherwise she cycles. When she cycles she is late 10% of the time. When she takes the bus she is late 20% of the time.

(a) Represent the given information on a tree diagram.

(b) Find the probability that she is late.

(c) Given that she is late, find the probability that she took the bus.

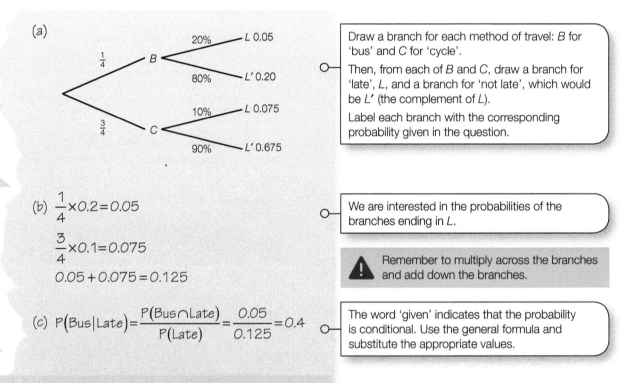

(a)

$\frac{1}{4}$ — B — 20% — L 0.05
— 80% — L' 0.20

$\frac{3}{4}$ — C — 10% — L 0.075
— 90% — L' 0.675

Draw a branch for each method of travel: B for 'bus' and C for 'cycle'.

Then, from each of B and C, draw a branch for 'late', L, and a branch for 'not late', which would be L' (the complement of L).

Label each branch with the corresponding probability given in the question.

(b) $\frac{1}{4} \times 0.2 = 0.05$

$\frac{3}{4} \times 0.1 = 0.075$

$0.05 + 0.075 = 0.125$

We are interested in the probabilities of the branches ending in L.

⚠ Remember to multiply across the branches and add down the branches.

(c) $P(\text{Bus}|\text{Late}) = \dfrac{P(\text{Bus} \cap \text{Late})}{P(\text{Late})} = \dfrac{0.05}{0.125} = 0.4$

The word 'given' indicates that the probability is conditional. Use the general formula and substitute the appropriate values.

Practice questions 6.4

7. 30% of widgets produced in a factory are made by Machine A. The remainder are made by Machine B. One third of widgets produced by Machine A are faulty. One fifth of widgets produced by Machine B are faulty. Find the probability that a randomly chosen widget from the factory is faulty.

8. 24% of people have the gene *lepA*. Of those with the gene, 12% have diabetes. Of those without the gene, 8% have diabetes.

(a) Represent the given information on a tree diagram.

(b) Find the probability that a randomly chosen person has diabetes.

(c) If a person has diabetes, find the probability that they have the *lepA* gene.

6.5 VENN DIAGRAMS

WORKED EXAMPLE 6.5

60% of students have a laptop and 50% have a television. 40% of students have both.

(a) Represent the given information on a Venn diagram.

(b) Find the probability that a student has either a television or a laptop.

(c) Given that a student has a laptop, find the probability that they have a television.

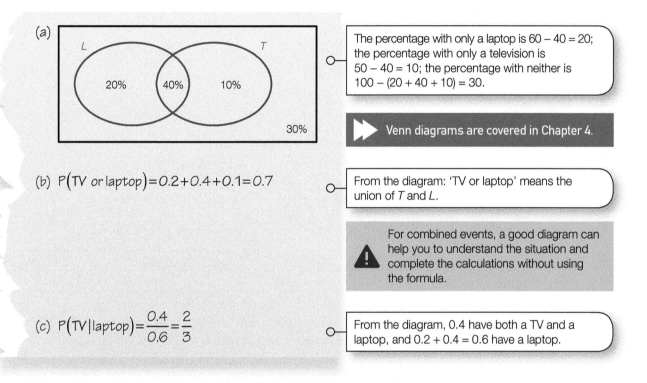

(a)

The percentage with only a laptop is 60 − 40 = 20; the percentage with only a television is 50 − 40 = 10; the percentage with neither is 100 − (20 + 40 + 10) = 30.

▶ Venn diagrams are covered in Chapter 4.

(b) $P(\text{TV or laptop}) = 0.2 + 0.4 + 0.1 = 0.7$

From the diagram: 'TV or laptop' means the union of T and L.

⚠ For combined events, a good diagram can help you to understand the situation and complete the calculations without using the formula.

(c) $P(\text{TV}\,|\,\text{laptop}) = \dfrac{0.4}{0.6} = \dfrac{2}{3}$

From the diagram, 0.4 have both a TV and a laptop, and 0.2 + 0.4 = 0.6 have a laptop.

Practice questions 6.5

9. In a library, $\dfrac{3}{5}$ of the books are fiction and $\dfrac{2}{3}$ are set in Europe. One half of the books are fiction set in Europe.

    (a) Represent the given information on a Venn diagram.

    (b) If a book is chosen at random, calculate the probability that:

        (i) the book is either fiction or set in Europe

        (ii) the book is neither fiction nor set in Europe

        (iii) the book is fiction given that it is set in Europe.

10. 60% of the apps on Leila's computer are educational and 80% are free. If all of her apps are either educational or free, find the probability that a randomly chosen app is:

    (a) educational and free

    (b) educational given that it is free.

Mixed practice 6

1. A bag contains 10 red marbles and 14 green marbles.
   (a) If one marble is chosen at random, find the probability that it is red.
   (b) If two marbles are chosen at random without replacement, find the probability that they are:
      (i) both red   (ii) different colours.

2. The following table shows the results of a football team during one season.

		Result		
		Lose	Draw	Win
Goals scored	0	8	6	0
	1	8	10	6
	>1	1	3	5

   (a) How many games did the team play in this season?
   (b) Use the results from this season to estimate the probability of the team:
      (i) winning
      (ii) scoring more than one goal
      (iii) winning given that more than one goal was scored
      (iv) drawing given that at least one goal was scored.

    In conditional probability the denominator will change depending on the conditions.

3. In Geometon, the probability of it raining on any given day is 40%, independent of any other day. If it rains, the probability that Juan takes an umbrella is 0.8. If it is not raining, the probability that Juan takes his umbrella is 0.3.
   (a) What is the probability that it rains on two consecutive days?
   (b) What is the probability that Juan takes his umbrella?

4. A spinner is labelled with four prizes: a chocolate, a sweet, a crayon and a ball.
   (a) Find the value of x.
   (b) Find the probability of winning a ball.
   (c) Given that a prize is won, find the probability of winning a ball.

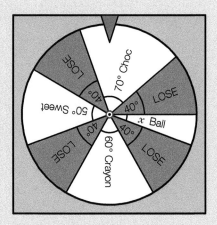

5. On a TV channel, 40% of shows are dramas and 60% are set in America. 30% of the shows are dramas set in America.

(a) Draw a Venn diagram to represent this information.

(b) Find the probability that a randomly selected show is a drama not set in America.

(c) If a randomly selected show is set in America, find the probability that it is a drama.

6. The table below shows how students in a school year are grouped.

		Group A	Group B	Group C
Sex	Male	10	13	13
	Female	12	11	15

(a) How many students are in the school year?

(b) If a student is chosen at random, calculate the probability that the student is:

    (i) female

    (ii) male and from group C

    (iii) female or from group B.

(c) All the male students are put in a room. One of these students is chosen at random. What is the probability that the student is from group A?

(d) Two pupils are chosen at random. What is the probability that they are both from group C?

Going for the top 6

1. 30% of clothes sold by a shop are pink and 60% are dresses. Given that the colour of the item sold is independent of whether or not it is a dress, find the proportion of clothes sold in the shop which are neither pink nor dresses.

2. A bag contains 12 red balls, 20 green balls and 18 blue balls.

(a) If three balls are picked at random, find the probability that they are all the same colour.

(b) If three balls are picked at random, find the probability that they are all different colours.

(c) Given that the first two balls picked are blue, find the probability that the third ball picked is blue.

(d) Find the probability that the third ball picked is red.

7 STATISTICAL APPLICATIONS

- The normal distribution is used to model continuous random variables. To work with the normal distribution you need to know the mean (μ) and standard deviation (σ) of the population from which the data is being collected.

  - If a random variable follows a normal distribution, approximately 68% of the values lie between $\mu - \sigma$ and $\mu + \sigma$; approximately 95% lie between $\mu - 2\sigma$ and $\mu + 2\sigma$; and approximately 99% lie between $\mu - 3\sigma$ and $\mu + 3\sigma$.

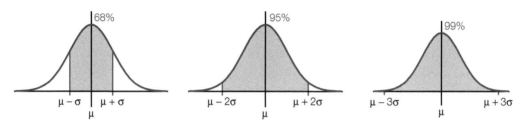

- A GDC can be used for probability calculations involving the normal distribution.

- An inverse normal calculation gives the value on the x-axis corresponding to the given probability of being below that x value.

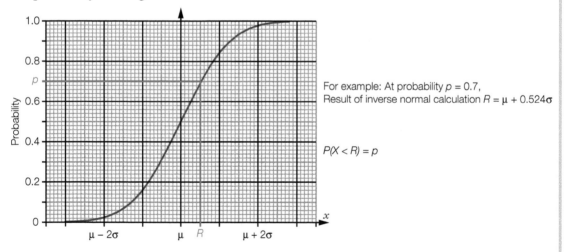

For example: At probability $p = 0.7$,
Result of inverse normal calculation $R = \mu + 0.524\sigma$

$P(X < R) = p$

- The relationship between two variables is referred to as the correlation. Correlation does not imply causation.

  - Scatter diagrams help to illustrate the connection between two variables.

  - Pearson's product–moment correlation coefficient, r, is a measure of the linear correlation between two variables. It can take any value between -1 and $+1$. Its sign indicates the type of correlation, and its magnitude indicates the strength of the correlation.

    - A value of r close to -1 shows that there is a strong negative correlation. A value close to $+1$ shows that there is a strong positive correlation, and a value close to 0 shows no linear correlation.

- The regression line is a line of best fit describing a linear relationship between two variables.

  - The regression line passes through the mean point $(\overline{x}, \overline{y})$.

  - The equation of the regression line can be used to estimate values that are not in the original data. Such an estimate is reliable only if the correlation is strong and the values of the variables are within the range of the original data.

- The chi-squared (χ^2) test is used to determine whether two quantities are independent, based on information (observed frequencies) given in a contingency table.

  - The expected frequencies can be calculated from the table using the formula:
  $$\text{expected frequency} = \frac{\text{row total} \times \text{column total}}{\text{total}}.$$

- To conduct a χ^2 test:

  - State the null hypothesis (H_0) and alternative hypothesis (H_1). H_0 always assumes that the two variables are independent.

  - Find the number of degrees of freedom using the formula:
  degrees of freedom = (number of rows − 1) × (number of columns − 1)

  - Identify the critical value of χ^2 or the significance level (which will be given in the question).

  - Find the chi-squared statistic (χ^2_{calc}) or the p-value for the data (using a GDC).

  - State the conclusion of the test:

    - If $\chi^2_{calc} > \chi^2_{critical}$, or if the p-value is less than the significance level, reject H_0 and conclude that the two variables are dependent.

    - If $\chi^2_{calc} < \chi^2_{critical}$, or if the p-value is greater than the significance level, there is not enough evidence to reject H_0, so conclude that the two variables are independent.

⚠ EXAM TIPS AND COMMON ERRORS

- When doing calculations with the normal distribution, it is always a good idea to draw a clear diagram showing the area that you are using to solve the problem.
- In the exam you will be expected to use a GDC to find Pearson's product–moment correlation coefficient and the regression line.
- The expected frequencies for the χ^2 test can be found using a GDC, but you also need to know how to calculate them from a contingency table.
- In the exam you will be expected to do the calculations for a χ^2 test on your GDC. The questions will test your understanding of the results that your calculator produces.
- In a χ^2 test, the hypotheses and the conclusion must always refer to the context of the question.

7.1 THE NORMAL DISTRIBUTION

WORKED EXAMPLE 7.1

The heights of rose bushes are normally distributed with mean 87 cm and standard deviation 6 cm.

(a) 28% of rose bushes are taller than k cm. Determine the value of k.

(b) 26 rose bushes are selected at random. How many would be expected to have a height of between 78 cm and 90 cm?

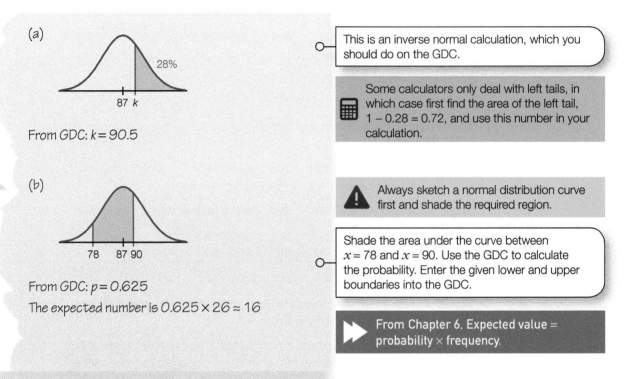

(a)

28%

87 k

From GDC: $k = 90.5$

This is an inverse normal calculation, which you should do on the GDC.

Some calculators only deal with left tails, in which case first find the area of the left tail, $1 - 0.28 = 0.72$, and use this number in your calculation.

(b)

78 87 90

From GDC: $p = 0.625$

The expected number is $0.625 \times 26 \approx 16$

Always sketch a normal distribution curve first and shade the required region.

Shade the area under the curve between $x = 78$ and $x = 90$. Use the GDC to calculate the probability. Enter the given lower and upper boundaries into the GDC.

From Chapter 6. Expected value = probability × frequency.

Practice questions 7.1

1. The masses of kittens are normally distributed with mean 1.2 kg and standard deviation 0.3 kg.
    (a) Out of a group of 20 kittens, how many would be expected to have a mass of less than 1 kg?
    (b) 30% of kittens have a mass of more than m kg. Determine the value of m.

2. The random variable X is normally distributed with mean 3 and standard deviation 1.5.
    (a) Sketch the normal distribution diagram and shade the area corresponding to $P(2.6 < X < 3.7)$.
    (b) By considering a similar diagram, find the value of k such that $P(2.6 < X < k) = 0.52$.

7.2 PEARSON'S PRODUCT–MOMENT CORRELATION COEFFICIENT, r

WORKED EXAMPLE 7.2

The following table shows the outside temperatures and the amount of money taken by a hot chocolate machine, recorded on nine randomly selected days.

Temperature, T (°C)	23	12	5	8	16	−4	1	−2	9
Sales, S ($)	72	112	142	148	85	161	170	132	85

Calculate the value of Pearson's product–moment correlation coefficient for the data, and comment on the value of r.

 If an exam question asks for the product–moment correlation coefficient, you are expected to use your GDC.

From GDC: $r = -0.832$

The value of r is close to −1, showing that there is strong negative correlation between the outside temperature and sales of hot chocolate. As the outside temperature decreases, the sales of hot chocolate increase.

 You must refer to the context of the question when interpreting the value of r.

Practice questions 7.2

3. The following table shows the English and History test marks obtained by a class of eight students.

History mark (%)	62	48	82	71	53	67	90	56
English mark (%)	54	71	52	46	85	72	76	82

Calculate Pearson's product–moment correlation coefficient, r, for the data and comment on what the value of r suggests about the relationship between the History and English marks.

4. Jack and Jill collected some data on people's salaries and the value of the cars they own. They calculated the product–moment correlation coefficient for the data, and found that $r = 0.863$. They then tried to interpret what this value meant. State whether each interpretation is correct, giving a reason for your answer.

    (a) Jack says: 'If a person has a higher salary, they can be expected to have a more expensive car.'

    (b) Jill says: 'An increase in salary would cause a person to buy a more expensive car.'

7.3 REGRESSION LINE OF y ON x

WORKED EXAMPLE 7.3

Using the data from Worked Example 7.2:

(a) Find the equation of the regression line of S on T.

(b) Estimate the outside temperature on a day when the total sales of hot chocolate are $120.

(c) The regression line is used to estimate the sales of hot chocolate on a day when the outside temperature is 35°C. Comment on the reliability of this estimate.

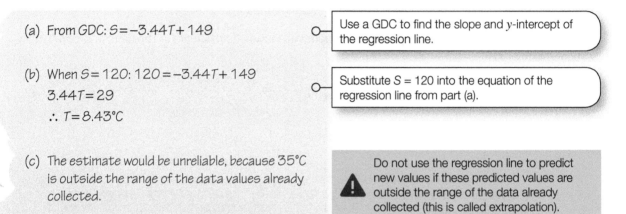

(a) From GDC: $S = -3.44T + 149$

> Use a GDC to find the slope and y-intercept of the regression line.

(b) When $S = 120$: $120 = -3.44T + 149$

$3.44T = 29$

$\therefore T = 8.43°C$

> Substitute $S = 120$ into the equation of the regression line from part (a).

(c) The estimate would be unreliable, because 35°C is outside the range of the data values already collected.

> ⚠ Do not use the regression line to predict new values if these predicted values are outside the range of the data already collected (this is called extrapolation).

Practice questions 7.3

5. (a) Find the equation of the regression line of y on x for the data in the table below.

x	2.7	6.3	1.4	1.9	3.6	7.4	4.1	5.3
y	0.28	0.60	0.25	0.26	0.33	0.59	0.33	0.61

(b) Estimate the value of x when $y = 0.52$.

6. The managers of two companies want to see whether there is any correlation between the age (A) and salary (S) of their employees. The employees in the sample are aged between 16 and 42.

(a) The first manager finds that the correlation coefficient of the data A and S is 0.872 and the equation of the regression line is $S = 1000A + 2000$. He uses the equation to estimate salaries for given ages. For each of the values of A below, either estimate the salary or explain why the estimate would not be reliable.

    (i) $A = 37$ (ii) $A = 56$

(b) The second manager finds that the correlation coefficient is -0.217 and the equation of the regression line is $S = -502A + 2720$. He uses this equation to estimate the salary of a 25-year-old employee. Comment on the reliability of this estimate, giving reasons for your answer.

7.4 THE CHI-SQUARED TEST FOR INDEPENDENCE

WORKED EXAMPLE 7.4

A teacher wants to investigate whether the IB Maths grade of a student is dependent on gender. The table shows the grades of a sample of 110 students.

The teacher carries out a chi-squared test at the 5% significance level.

	Grade			
	4	5	6	7
Male	12	18	23	10
Female	9	15	16	7

(a) State a suitable null hypothesis and an alternative hypothesis.
(b) Calculate the expected frequency of female students getting a grade 5, showing all your working.
(c) Determine the chi-squared statistic for this data, and state the number of degrees of freedom.
(d) The χ^2 critical value is 7.815. What conclusion can be drawn from this test? Give a reason for your answer.

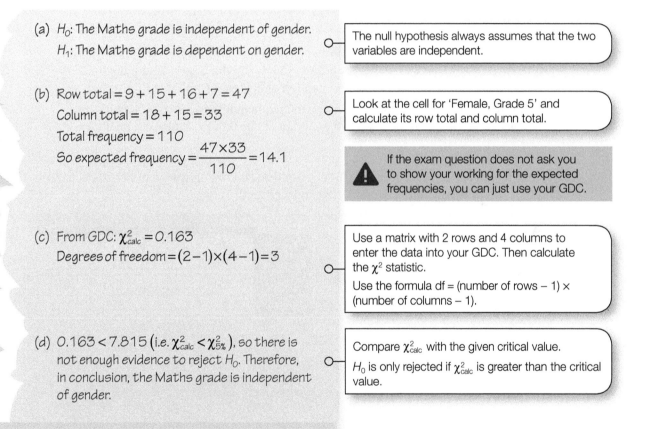

(a) H_0: The Maths grade is independent of gender.
H_1: The Maths grade is dependent on gender.

○— The null hypothesis always assumes that the two variables are independent.

(b) Row total $= 9 + 15 + 16 + 7 = 47$
Column total $= 18 + 15 = 33$
Total frequency $= 110$
So expected frequency $= \dfrac{47 \times 33}{110} = 14.1$

○— Look at the cell for 'Female, Grade 5' and calculate its row total and column total.

⚠ If the exam question does not ask you to show your working for the expected frequencies, you can just use your GDC.

(c) From GDC: $\chi^2_{calc} = 0.163$
Degrees of freedom $= (2-1) \times (4-1) = 3$

○— Use a matrix with 2 rows and 4 columns to enter the data into your GDC. Then calculate the χ^2 statistic.
Use the formula df = (number of rows − 1) × (number of columns − 1).

(d) $0.163 < 7.815$ (i.e. $\chi^2_{calc} < \chi^2_{5\%}$), so there is not enough evidence to reject H_0. Therefore, in conclusion, the Maths grade is independent of gender.

○— Compare χ^2_{calc} with the given critical value.
H_0 is only rejected if χ^2_{calc} is greater than the critical value.

Practice questions 7.4

7. Data on the gender and favourite colour of a group of 50 children is summarised in the contingency table.

	Red	Blue	Green
Boy	13	26	18
Girl	31	18	12

(a) State a suitable null hypothesis and an alternative hypothesis for a test to determine whether favourite colour is dependent on gender.

(b) Find the expected frequencies, the chi-squared statistic and the p-value for this test.

(c) What conclusion can be drawn from this test at the 10% significance level? Give a reason for your answer.

 An exam question may simply ask you to carry out a hypothesis test for independence. In that case you should follow all the steps as in question 7.

8. Tanya wants to test whether the length of a dog's tail is related to its colour. She decides to carry out a chi-squared test at the 1% significance level.

(a) State suitable hypotheses for this test.

(b) Each dog's colour is classified as brown, yellow or white, and the tail length is classified as long or short. Find the number of degrees of freedom for this test.

(c) Tanya collected information on colour and tail length for 60 dogs. Using her calculator, she found the p-value for this data to be 0.0152. State her conclusion.

9. A teacher has collected data on the favourite subject and first language of her students, in order to test whether the two variables are independent.

(a) Find the values A, B, C and D in the table.

(b) The expected frequency for the number of Spanish speakers who prefer History is 18.9. Show how this value was calculated.

	Biology	History	Maths	Totals
Chinese	26	38	51	A
English	62	18	C	97
Spanish	12	32	D	B
Totals	100	88	82	270

(c) The critical value for the chi-squared test at the 5% significance level is 9.48. Use this to decide whether favourite subject is independent of first language.

! An exam question will always give you the critical value of χ^2 that you need.

Mixed practice 7

1. Match each diagram with the most appropriate value of Pearson's product–moment correlation coefficient.

   (a) $r = 0.932$ (b) $r = -0.561$ (c) $r = 0.125$

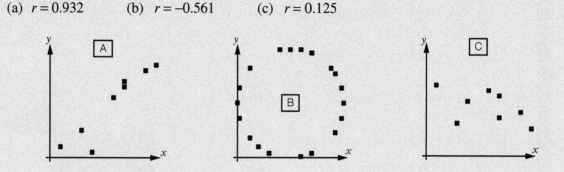

2. The following table shows the masses (m kg) and lengths (l cm) of 11 babies.

m	2.7	4.3	3.4	2.9	3.6	4.7	4.1	3.3	3.1	4.3	3.7
l	48	55	52	47	51	56	53	51	50	51	49

   (a) Write down the correlation coefficient, r, of the data.

   (b) Find the equation of the regression line of l on m.

   (c) Use your equation to estimate the length of a baby whose mass is 3.2 kg.

   (d) Can the regression line be reliably used to estimate the length of a baby of mass 5.6 kg? Explain your answer.

3. The masses of dogs of a certain breed are normally distributed with mean 4.6 kg and standard deviation 1.2 kg.

   (a) A dog is chosen at random. Find the probability that it has a mass of:

      (i) between 3.2 kg and 4.8 kg

      (ii) more than 5.0 kg.

   (b) Two dogs are chosen at random. What is the probability that exactly one of them has a mass of more than 5.0 kg?

4. The times taken to travel to school for a sample of 40 students are summarised in the table.

Time (minutes)	0–5	5–10	10–15	15–20	20–25
Frequency	3	9	13	10	5

   (a) Find the mean and standard deviation of the times.

The times for the whole school follow a normal distribution with mean 16 minutes and standard deviation 6 minutes.

(b) The results from this sample are used to approximate the mean and standard deviation of the times for the whole school. Find the percentage error in this approximation.

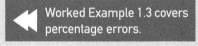
Worked Example 1.3 covers percentage errors.

(c) What percentage of students take more than half an hour to travel to school?

5. The table shows the eye colour and hair colour of 228 children.

		Hair colour	
		Fair	Dark
Eye colour	Blue	32	54
	Green	18	32
	Brown	21	71

(a) Find the probability that a child has:

   (i) fair hair and brown eyes

   (ii) dark hair.

(b) State suitable hypotheses for a chi-squared test to determine whether hair colour and eye colour are independent.

(c) Carry out the test at the 5% significance level, showing all your working and clearly stating your conclusion.

6. The lengths (l cm) and widths (w cm) of eight leaves of a certain plant are given in the table and plotted on the scatter diagram.

l	w
7.3	5.6
8.5	6.7
8.6	6.3
7.6	5.5
6.2	4.1
6.9	5.2
7.7	B
A	5.9

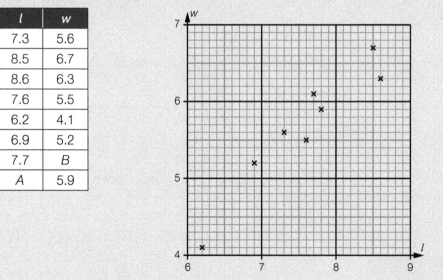

(a) Describe the relationship between the length and width of a leaf.

(b) Fill in the missing information in the table.

(c) Calculate the mean length and mean width, and mark this point on the scatter diagram.

(d) Draw a line of best fit on the diagram.

Going for the top 7

1. The random variable X is normally distributed with mean 5.

    (a) Sketch and label a normal distribution diagram to show this information.

    (b) Given that $P(X < 3) = 0.06$, find $P(5 < X < 7)$.

2. A sports club recorded the amount of money they spent on advertising (a USD) over a period of several years together with the number of members (M). They found that there is a strong correlation between the two, and that the equation of the regression line is $M = 123 + 2.6a$.

    (a) How much money does the club need to spend on advertising if they want 250 members?

    (b) What does the number 123 in the equation of the regression line represent?

3. The table shows the nationality and the favourite sport of a group of 242 students.

    (a) A test is to be carried out to determine whether the favourite sport is dependent on nationality. State the name of this test, and write down suitable hypotheses.

		Favourite sport	
		Basketball	Soccer
Nationality	Brazilian	26	54
	Mexican	31	47
	Indian	51	33

    (b) Find the probability that a student:

       (i) is Brazilian

      (ii) prefers basketball.

    (c) **Hence** explain why the expected frequency for the cell in the first row and first column is 35.7, assuming that the favourite sport is independent of nationality.

    (d) Carry out the hypothesis test at the 10% significance level, clearly stating your conclusion.

4. The test scores of a group of 120 students are shown in the frequency histogram below.

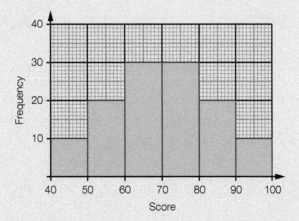

    (a) Estimate the mean and the standard deviation of the test scores.

    (b) Estimate the number of students whose test score is within one standard deviation of the mean.

    (c) **Hence** explain whether a normal distribution would be a suitable model for these test scores.

8 GEOMETRY AND TRIGONOMETRY

WHAT YOU NEED TO KNOW

- A straight line has equation $y = mx + c$ or $ax + by + d = 0$.
  - If a line passes through two points (x_1, y_1) and (x_2, y_2), the gradient of the line is $m = \dfrac{y_2 - y_1}{x_2 - x_1}$.
  - The equation of the line can be found by writing $y - y_1 = m(x - x_1)$ and substituting in the values of m, x_1 and y_1.
  - Parallel lines have the same gradient, $m_1 = m_2$.
  - Two lines are perpendicular if their gradients satisfy $m_1 m_2 = -1$ or, equivalently, $m_2 = -\dfrac{1}{m_1}$.

- In a right-angled triangle ABC:
  - $c^2 = a^2 + b^2$ (Pythagoras' theorem)
  - $\sin A = \dfrac{a}{c}$, $\cos A = \dfrac{b}{c}$, $\tan A = \dfrac{a}{b}$
    where a is the side opposite the given angle A, b is the side adjacent to it, and c is the hypotenuse.

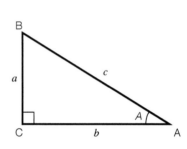

- Right-angled triangles can be used to find angles of elevation and depression.

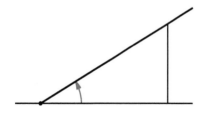

Angle of elevation

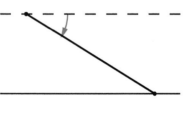

Angle of depression

- In any triangle ABC:

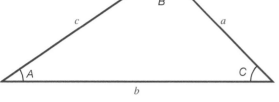

- The sine rule states that $\dfrac{a}{\sin A} = \dfrac{b}{\sin B} = \dfrac{c}{\sin C}$

  - The sine rule is used when a side and the angle opposite are known.

- The cosine rule states that:

$$a^2 = b^2 + c^2 - 2bc\cos A$$

$$\cos A = \frac{b^2 + c^2 - a^2}{2bc}$$

  - The first form is used to find the length of an unknown side when two sides and the angle between them are known.

  - The second form is used to find an angle when all three sides are known.

  - Any triangle can be relabelled to get the correct sides in the correct places.

- The area of triangle ABC is given by

  $\text{Area} = \dfrac{1}{2}ab\sin C$ where a and b are adjacent sides and C is the included angle.

- Lengths and angles in three-dimensional shapes can be found by using right-angled triangles.

  - To find distances between points, Pythagoras' theorem can be used several times. Alternatively, it is useful to remember that:

  $$\text{distance } d = \sqrt{(\text{horizontal distance})^2 + (\text{vertical distance})^2 + (\text{depth})^2}$$

- The volume and surface area formulae for the solids below, with the exception of the hemisphere, are given in the Formula booklet:

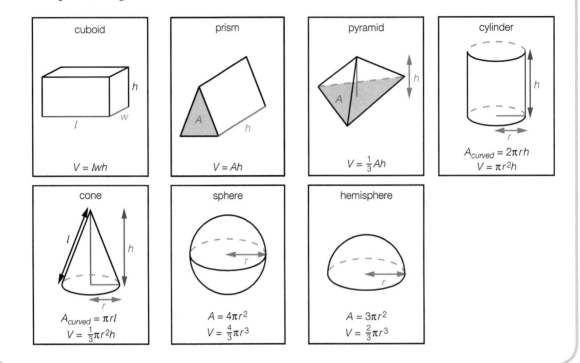

cuboid	prism	pyramid	cylinder
$V = lwh$	$V = Ah$	$V = \frac{1}{3}Ah$	$A_{curved} = 2\pi rh$ $V = \pi r^2 h$

cone	sphere	hemisphere
$A_{curved} = \pi rl$ $V = \frac{1}{3}\pi r^2 h$	$A = 4\pi r^2$ $V = \frac{4}{3}\pi r^3$	$A = 3\pi r^2$ $V = \frac{2}{3}\pi r^3$

⚠ EXAM TIPS AND COMMON ERRORS

- Always sketch and label clear diagrams. For long questions, add information to the diagram as you work through the question.

- Students often use the sine and cosine rules in right-angled triangles – this gives the right answer but is unnecessarily complicated.

- Be careful when doing calculations with the cosine rule. You should enter the whole calculation into your GDC at once, and use brackets, i.e. $\cos A = \dfrac{(b^2 + c^2 - a^2)}{(2 \times b \times c)}$.

- Before doing any calculations, make sure your GDC is in degree mode. If you reset your calculator, it will change the angle measurement to radians.

- Make sure you include units with your final answer, and give all answers correct to three significant figures.

- You do not need to include units in your working.

- Do not round intermediate answers; store them in the calculator memory to avoid rounding errors in future calculations.

8.1 EQUATION OF A STRAIGHT LINE

WORKED EXAMPLE 8.1

(a) Find the equation of the straight line passing through the points A(−2, 3) and B(4, −7).
Give your answer in the form $ax + by + c = 0$, where $a, b, c \in \mathbb{Z}$.

(b) Find the equation of the line perpendicular to AB that passes through the origin.

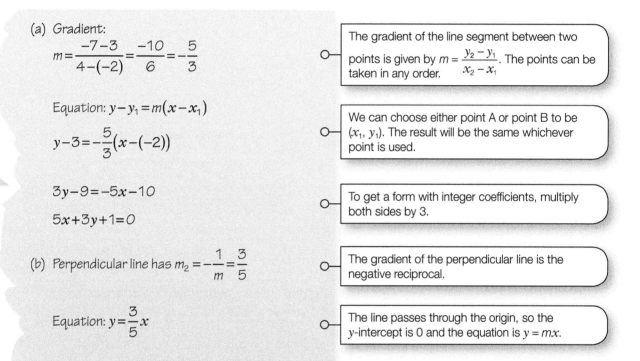

(a) Gradient:
$$m = \frac{-7-3}{4-(-2)} = \frac{-10}{6} = -\frac{5}{3}$$

The gradient of the line segment between two points is given by $m = \frac{y_2 - y_1}{x_2 - x_1}$. The points can be taken in any order.

Equation: $y - y_1 = m(x - x_1)$
$$y - 3 = -\frac{5}{3}(x - (-2))$$

We can choose either point A or point B to be (x_1, y_1). The result will be the same whichever point is used.

$$3y - 9 = -5x - 10$$
$$5x + 3y + 1 = 0$$

To get a form with integer coefficients, multiply both sides by 3.

(b) Perpendicular line has $m_2 = -\frac{1}{m} = \frac{3}{5}$

The gradient of the perpendicular line is the negative reciprocal.

Equation: $y = \frac{3}{5}x$

The line passes through the origin, so the y-intercept is 0 and the equation is $y = mx$.

Practice questions 8.1

1. Find the equation of the line shown in the diagram.

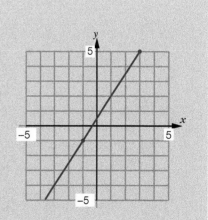

2. The line l_1 passes through the point (4, −3) and has gradient $\frac{1}{2}$.
   (a) Find the equation of l_1 in the form $y = mx + c$.
   (b) The line l_2 has equation $2x + y = 7$. Are l_1 and l_2 perpendicular? Explain your answer.

8.2 RIGHT-ANGLED TRIANGLES

WORKED EXAMPLE 8.2

Robert observes a ship from a cliff. The ship is 1.3 km away from the bottom of the cliff. Given that the height of the cliff is 150 m, find the angle of depression of the ship.

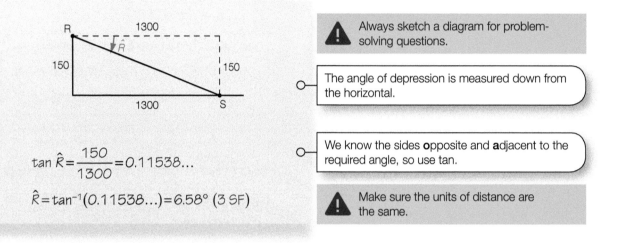

$$\tan \hat{R} = \frac{150}{1300} = 0.11538...$$

$$\hat{R} = \tan^{-1}(0.11538...) = 6.58° \text{ (3 SF)}$$

> ⚠ Always sketch a diagram for problem-solving questions.

> The angle of depression is measured down from the horizontal.

> We know the sides **o**pposite and **a**djacent to the required angle, so use tan.

> ⚠ Make sure the units of distance are the same.

Practice questions 8.2

3. Bea observes a tree. She stands 8 m away from the base of the tree. Given that the height of the tree is 18 m, find the angle of elevation from Bea to the top of the tree.

4. From the top of a lighthouse, the angle of depression of a boat is 6°. The horizontal distance between the boat and the bottom of the lighthouse is 750 m. Find:
   (a) the distance of the boat from the top of the lighthouse
   (b) the vertical height of the lighthouse.

5. A rectangle has sides x cm and $(x + 2)$ cm, and its diagonals have length $(x + 5)$ cm.
   (a) Find the value of x.
   (b) Find the angle between a diagonal and a long side of the rectangle.

6. Alice observes a nearby tree from her house. From ground level, the angle of elevation of the top of the tree is 52°. From the first-floor window, which is 3.5 m above the ground, the angle of depression of the bottom of the tree is 9°.
   (a) Find the distance, d, between the house and the tree.
   (b) Find the height of the tree.

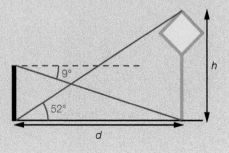

8.3 NON-RIGHT-ANGLED TRIANGLES

WORKED EXAMPLE 8.3

For the triangle shown in the diagram:

(a) Find the size of angle
    (i) $A\hat{B}C$ (ii) $B\hat{C}A$

(b) Find the area of triangle ABC.

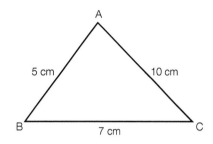

(a) (i) $\cos B = \dfrac{a^2 + c^2 - b^2}{2ac}$

         $= \dfrac{7^2 + 5^2 - 10^2}{2 \times 7 \times 5}$

         $= -0.3714\ldots$

    $B = \cos^{-1}(0.3714) = 112°$ (3 SF)

> We are given the lengths of three sides, so use the cosine rule.

> Do not round the intermediate answer – use the ANS button on your GDC.

(ii) $\dfrac{\sin C}{c} = \dfrac{\sin B}{b}$

    $\dfrac{\sin C}{5} = \dfrac{\sin 112°}{10} = 0.09284\ldots$

    $\sin C = 5 \times 0.09284\ldots = 0.4642\ldots$

    $C = \sin^{-1}(0.4642\ldots) = 27.7°$

> Since we now know angle B, we can use the sine rule.

(b) Area $= \dfrac{1}{2}ab\sin C$

          $= \dfrac{1}{2}(10 \times 7)\sin 27.7°$

          $= 16.2\,\text{cm}^2$

> Here, we can use any of the angles and the adjacent sides in the area formula. Since we have just calculated angle C in part (a)(ii), we will use that one.

> The formula for the area of a triangle always uses two sides and the included angle.

Practice questions 8.3

7. The triangle shown in the diagram has area 22.6 cm².

   (a) Find the size of the acute angle $P\hat{Q}R$.

   (b) Find the length of the side PR.

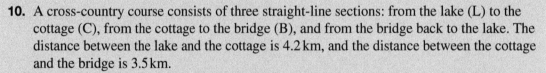

8. In triangle ABC, AB = 6 cm, BC = 11 cm and angle $B\hat{A}C = 42°$. Find:

   (a) the size of angle $A\hat{C}B$

   (b) the length CA

   (c) the area of triangle ABC.

9. In the diagram shown, ACD is an isosceles triangle with

$A\hat{D}C = C\hat{A}D = 35°$ and AD = 18 cm.

   (a) Write down the size of angle $A\hat{C}D$ and find the length CD.

   (b) Given that BC = 7 cm, find the perimeter of triangle ABD.

10. A cross-country course consists of three straight-line sections: from the lake (L) to the cottage (C), from the cottage to the bridge (B), and from the bridge back to the lake. The distance between the lake and the cottage is 4.2 km, and the distance between the cottage and the bridge is 3.5 km.

   (a) Sketch a diagram to represent the above information.

   (b) Given that the total length of the course is 8.8 km, find the size of angle $L\hat{C}B$.

11. The four sides of a field have lengths 240 m, 180 m, 200 m and x m, as shown in the diagram. Angle $R\hat{S}P = 56°$.

   (a) Calculate the area of triangle PRS.

The farmer builds a straight fence from P to R.

   (b) Find the length of the fence.

   (c) Given that the fence divides the field into two parts of equal area, find:

      (i) the acute angle $Q\hat{P}R$ (ii) the length x.

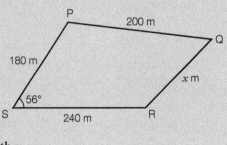

8.4 TRIGONOMETRY AND THREE-DIMENSIONAL SOLIDS

WORKED EXAMPLE 8.4

The base of a right pyramid is a square of side 6 cm. The length of
the edge AM is 9 cm.

(a) Find the length of the diagonal of the square.

(b) Find the vertical height of the pyramid.

(c) Find the angle that the line AM makes with the base.

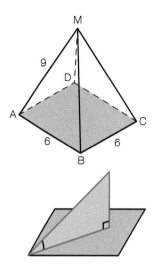

> ⚠ Exam questions on solids will be set so that you can answer
> them using right-angled triangles. Make a sketch of the
> appropriate triangle and mark the right angle clearly. To find
> the angle between an edge and a plane, draw a perpendicular
> line from the top of the edge to the plane.

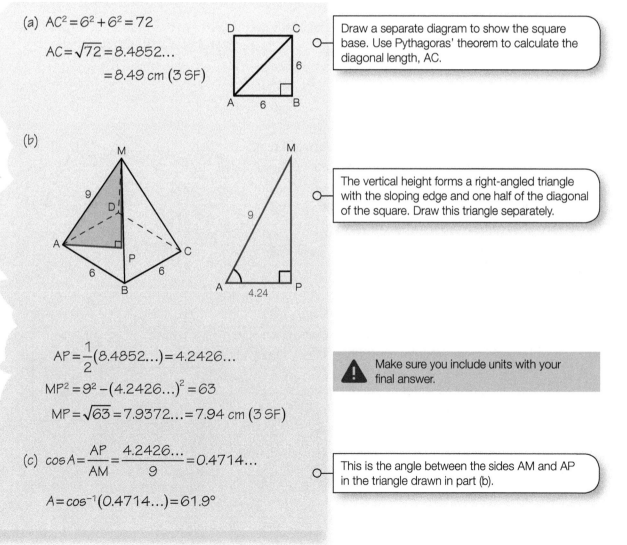

(a) $AC^2 = 6^2 + 6^2 = 72$

$AC = \sqrt{72} = 8.4852...$

$\quad = 8.49\ cm\ (3\ SF)$

> Draw a separate diagram to show the square
> base. Use Pythagoras' theorem to calculate the
> diagonal length, AC.

(b)

> The vertical height forms a right-angled triangle
> with the sloping edge and one half of the diagonal
> of the square. Draw this triangle separately.

$AP = \dfrac{1}{2}(8.4852...) = 4.2426...$

$MP^2 = 9^2 - (4.2426...)^2 = 63$

$MP = \sqrt{63} = 7.9372... = 7.94\ cm\ (3\ SF)$

> ⚠ Make sure you include units with your
> final answer.

(c) $\cos A = \dfrac{AP}{AM} = \dfrac{4.2426...}{9} = 0.4714...$

$A = \cos^{-1}(0.4714...) = 61.9°$

> This is the angle between the sides AM and AP
> in the triangle drawn in part (b).

Practice questions 8.4

12. The base of a right pyramid is a square, ABCD, of side 12 cm. The length of the edge AM is 21 cm.

    (a) Find the length of the diagonal of the square ABCD.

    (b) Find the vertical height of the pyramid.

    (c) Find the size of the angle between:

        (i) AM and MB   (ii) AM and AC.

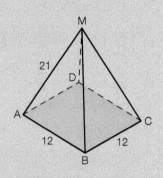

13. ABCDEFGH is a cuboid with sides of lengths 18 cm, 13 cm and 7 cm.

    (a) Find the length of

        (i) FH   (ii) FD.

    (b) Find the angle that the line FD makes with the base EFGH.

    (c) Find the angle between the diagonal FD and the side FB.

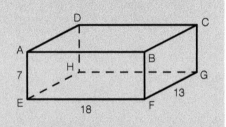

14. The base of a prism is an equilateral triangle with side 10 cm. The length of the prism is 23 cm.

    (a) Find the perpendicular height of the triangle.

    M is the midpoint of side AB.

    (b) Calculate the length MC.

    (c) Write down the size of angle $E\hat{M}C$.

    (d) Find the angle that the line EC makes with the plane ABCD.

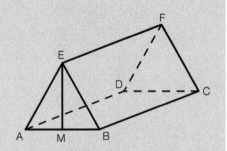

15. A room is in the shape of a cube with sides 4.5 m. The room is decorated using four ribbons attached to the centre of the ceiling and joined to the four corners of the floor.

    (a) Calculate the **total** length of ribbon.

    (b) Find the angle between:

        (i) two adjacent pieces of ribbon

        (ii) a piece of ribbon and the adjacent **vertical** edge of the cube.

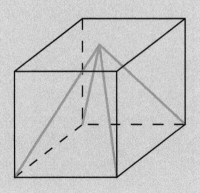

8.5 VOLUMES AND SURFACE AREAS OF THREE-DIMENSIONAL SOLIDS

WORKED EXAMPLE 8.5

The slant height of a cone is 12 cm, and the curved surface area is 208 cm². A hemisphere is attached to the base of the cone, as shown in the diagram.

Calculate the total surface area of the resulting solid.

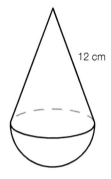

Curved surface area $= \pi r l$

$$208 = \pi r (12) \Rightarrow r = \frac{208}{12\pi} = 5.5173...$$

Total surface area $= \frac{1}{2}(4\pi r^2) + 208$

$$= 191.268... + 208 = 399 \text{ cm}^2$$

> First, we need to find the radius of the hemisphere (half a sphere), which is the same as the radius of the base of the cone.
>
> We find this by using the formula for the curved surface area of a cone.

Practice questions 8.5

16. Calculate the surface area of a cylinder of height 23 cm and volume 485 cm³.

17. A hemisphere of radius r cm is attached to one end of a cylinder of height $3r$ cm, as shown in the diagram.
   (a) Write an expression, in terms of r, for the surface area of the resulting solid.
   (b) Given that the solid has surface area 36π cm², find the value of r.
   (c) Find the volume of the solid.

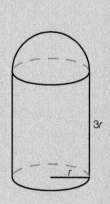

18. A cone has base radius 12 cm and volume 664 cm³. Find:
   (a) the vertical height
   (b) the total surface area of the cone.

19. The base of a prism is a right-angled triangle with sides 4 cm and 6 cm. The length of the prism is 11 cm.
   (a) Calculate the volume of the prism.
   (b) Find the length of the hypotenuse of the triangle, and the total surface area of the prism.

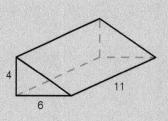

Mixed practice 8

1. C is the centre of a circle with radius 12 cm. A and B are two points on the circumference of the circle such that $A\hat{C}B = 120°$.

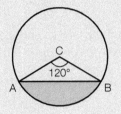

(a) Find the length of the chord AB.

(b) Calculate the shaded area.

(c) Celina estimates that the area of triangle ABC is about one sixth of the area of the circle. Find the percentage error in her estimate.

2. A solid cone has radius 9 cm and total surface area 707 cm².

(a) Find the slant height of the cone.

(b) Calculate the vertical height and the volume of the cone.

3. The base of a pyramid is a square with sides of length 8 cm. The triangular faces of the pyramid are isosceles triangles with sides of length 7 cm.

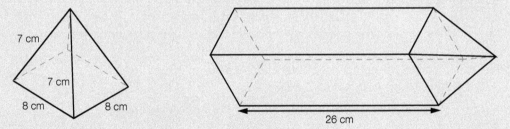

(a) Find the height and the area of each triangular face.

(b) Show that the height of the pyramid is 4.12 cm, correct to three significant figures.

The pyramid forms the lid of a pencil case. The total length of the pencil case is 26 cm.

(c) Find the total volume of the pencil case correct to three significant figures.

(d) The pencil case is coated in red material. By calculating surface areas, find the percentage of material which is used for the lid.

4. ABC is an equilateral triangle with side length 10 cm. P is a point on the side BC such that BP = x cm.

(a) Show that $AP^2 = x^2 - 10x + 100$.

(b) Find the values of x for which $AP = \sqrt{79}$ cm.

5. Two observers stand at points A and B on horizontal ground. The observer at A is 20 m away from a tree. The height of the tree is 16 m.

(a) Find the angle of elevation of the top of the tree from point A.

The angle of elevation of the top of the tree from point B is 32°.

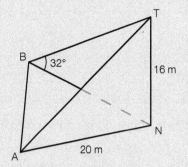

(b) Find the distance of B from the tree.

N is the point at the base of the tree. The distance between A and B is 12 m.

(c) Calculate the size of the angle $A\hat{N}B$.

6. The line l_1 has the equation $3x + 2y = 6$. It crosses the y-axis at the point M.

(a) Find:

    (i) the gradient of l_1 (ii) the coordinates of M.

The line l_2 passes through the point P(3, −8) and is perpendicular to the line l_1.

(b) Find the equation of l_2 in the form $ax + by + c = 0$.

The point of intersection of l_1 and l_2 is N.

(c) Find the coordinates of N.

(d) Calculate the distances NM and NP.

(e) Find the size of the angle $P\hat{M}N$.

(f) Find the area of triangle MNP.

Going for the top 8

1. A square-based pyramid has height 26 cm, and the sloping edges make a 72° angle with the base.

(a) Find the length of each sloping edge.

(b) Find the length of the diagonal of the square.

(c) Calculate the volume of the pyramid.

2. An open cylindrical cup has radius r and height h. The capacity of the cup is 200 cm³.

(a) Write an expression for h in terms of r.

(b) Hence show that the outer surface area of the cup is $S = \pi r^2 + \dfrac{400}{r}$.

(c) Find the value of r which gives the smallest possible surface area.

WHAT YOU NEED TO KNOW

- A function is a rule where for every input there is only one output.
    - The domain of a function is the set of allowed inputs.

    > ⚠ An exam question will either specify the domain of a function, or you should assume that the domain is all real numbers.

        - Some functions cannot have all real numbers in their domain; for example, you cannot divide by zero or take the square root of a negative number.
    - The range is the set of all possible outputs of a function. The easiest way of finding the range is to sketch the graph.
- Linear functions have the form $f(x) = mx + c$.
- Quadratic functions have the form $f(x) = ax^2 + bx + c$. The graph is a parabola.

    - The y-intercept of the graph, c, is found by setting $x = 0$.

    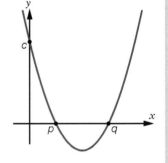

    > 🖩 After drawing the quadratic function $f(x) = ax^2 + bx + c$, you can use the graph to find the x-intercepts and hence solve the equation $ax^2 + bx + c = 0$, i.e. find the zeros or roots of the function.

    - The vertex of the parabola has x-coordinate $x = -\dfrac{b}{2a}$. This is also the equation of the line of symmetry of the graph. Substitute this value of x into the function to get the corresponding y-coordinate of the vertex.

- Exponential functions have the form $f(x) = ka^x + c$ (exponential growth) or $f(x) = ka^{-x} + c$ (exponential decay), where $a > 1$.

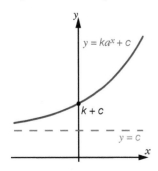 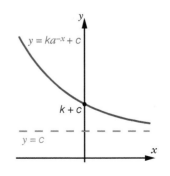

    - The y-intercept of the graph is $(0, k + c)$.
    It can also be found by setting $x = 0$ and remembering that $a^0 = 1$.

- The line $y = c$ is a horizontal asymptote. The graph approaches but never reaches this line.

 Calculators do not usually draw the asymptotes (as they are not a part of the graph). It is also easy to miss them if your viewing window is too large. This is why it is important to know which functions have asymptotes.

- Polynomial functions have the form $f(x) = ax^n + bx^m + \ldots$, where the powers of x are non-negative integers. The degree of the polynomial is the highest power that appears in the function's expression. A linear function is of degree 1, a quadratic function is of degree 2, and a cubic function is of degree 3.

- If a function of the form $f(x) = ax^n + bx^m + \ldots$ contains one or more powers of x that are negative integers, then $f(x)$ is a rational function. For example, $f(x) = x^2 + \dfrac{2}{x}$ contains a negative power of x (because $\dfrac{2}{x} = 2x^{-1}$) and can be written as $f(x) = \dfrac{x^3 + 2}{x}$, which is a ratio of two polynomials.

  - The graphs of such rational functions will have $x = 0$ (the y-axis) as a vertical asymptote.

- Equations can be solved using a number of different GDC options:

  - Equations of the form $f(x) = g(x)$ can be solved by plotting the graphs of $y = f(x)$ and $y = g(x)$ and finding the point(s) of intersection.

  - For an equation of the form $f(x) = 0$, the graph of $y = f(x)$ can be drawn to find the zeros (the solutions), or an equation solver can be used.

⚠ EXAM TIPS AND COMMON ERRORS

- You may be asked to 'sketch' or 'draw' a graph. A sketch only requires you to show the shape and main features of the graph, and you should always show the scale. A drawing must be a clearly labelled diagram or graph.

- Always substitute some numbers into the equation to make sure that your viewing window on the GDC is sensible. If you zoom in too much, the graph may look like a segment of straight line. If you zoom out too far, you may see nothing or just a vertical line. Students often think that their calculator is 'broken' when in fact they just haven't chosen a suitable viewing window.

- Sometimes equations will have parameters in place of coefficients (for example, $y = x^2 + k$). If you are not sure what the graph should look like, try sketching it for different values of the parameter (for example, $k = -1, 0, 2$).

- Be careful with negative powers. A common mistake is to think that $2x^{-2}$ is the same as $\dfrac{1}{2x^2}$ or $\dfrac{1}{4x^2}$; in fact it is $\dfrac{2}{x^2}$. Similarly, $\dfrac{1}{3x^2}$ is the same as $\dfrac{1}{3}x^{-2}$.

- Maximum and minimum points can also be found by using differentiation (see Chapter 10). If the question does not explicitly ask you to use differentiation, you can just read the coordinates of maximum and minimum points off the graph on your GDC.

9.1 USING THE GDC TO SOLVE EQUATIONS

WORKED EXAMPLE 9.1

Solve the equation $3^{-x} = 4 - x^2$.

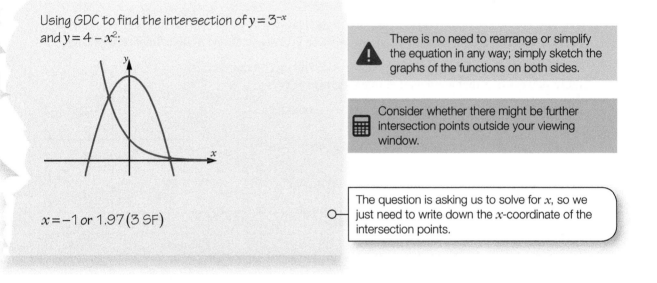

Using GDC to find the intersection of $y = 3^{-x}$ and $y = 4 - x^2$:

$x = -1$ or $1.97 \, (3 \, SF)$

> ⚠ There is no need to rearrange or simplify the equation in any way; simply sketch the graphs of the functions on both sides.

> 🖩 Consider whether there might be further intersection points outside your viewing window.

> The question is asking us to solve for x, so we just need to write down the x-coordinate of the intersection points.

Practice questions 9.1

> ⚠ Equations can usually be solved in more than one way using the GDC. Try to select the most appropriate method for each equation.

1. Solve the equation $5^x = x^3 + 2$.

2. Find all the solutions of the equation $x - \dfrac{1}{x} = 4 - x^2$.

3. The first term of a geometric series is 2 and the sum of the first four terms is 17. Find the value of the common ratio.

> ◀◀ Geometric sequences are covered in Chapter 2.

> 🖩 You can use the polynomial equation solver on your GDC, but the equation would first need to be rearranged into the form 'polynomial expression = 0'.

9.2 SOLVING PAIRS OF LINEAR EQUATIONS

WORKED EXAMPLE 9.2

A function is given by $g(x) = ax^3 - bx + 2$. Given that $g(-1) = 4$ and $g(2) = 16$, find the values of a and b.

$g(-1) = a(-1)^3 - b(-1) + 2 = 4 \Rightarrow -a + b = 2$
$g(2) = a(2)^3 - b(2) + 2 = 16 \Rightarrow 8a - 2b = 14$

Find $g(-1)$ and $g(2)$ to form a pair of linear equations.

From GDC: $a = 3$, $b = 5$

To solve a pair of linear equations using a graph, both equations must be put in the form $y = mx + c$. To solve using an equation solver, the correct form is $ax + by = c$.

Practice questions 9.2

4. The graph of the function $f(x) = A \times 3^x + k$ passes through the points $(1, 16)$ and $(2, 46)$. Find the values of A and k.

5. Find the coordinates of the point of intersection of the lines with equations $3x - 4y = 7$ and $11x + 5y = 74$.

6. The fifth term of an arithmetic sequence is 25 and the 18th term is 64. Find the first term and the common difference of the sequence.

 Arithmetic sequences are covered in Chapter 2.

7. A function $f(x) = ax^4 + bx + 1$ satisfies $f(2) = 42$ and $f'(2) = 21$. Find the values of a and b.

Differentiation is covered in Chapter 10.

8. A bag of rice costs r dollars and a loaf of bread costs b dollars. Samir orders 26 bags of rice and 42 loaves of bread for his restaurant, and pays 272 dollars.

(a) Write an equation to represent the information given.

Anita buys 2 bags of rice and 7 loaves of bread for her party. She spends 26 dollars.

(b) Find the price of a loaf of bread.

9.3 DOMAIN AND RANGE

WORKED EXAMPLE 9.3

A function is defined by $g(x) = (x - 1)^2 + 5$. Find the range of $g(x)$ if its domain is:

(a) $0 \leq x < 4$ (b) $x \in \{0, 1, 2, 3\}$

⚠️ The easiest way to find the range is to draw a graph or a mapping diagram.

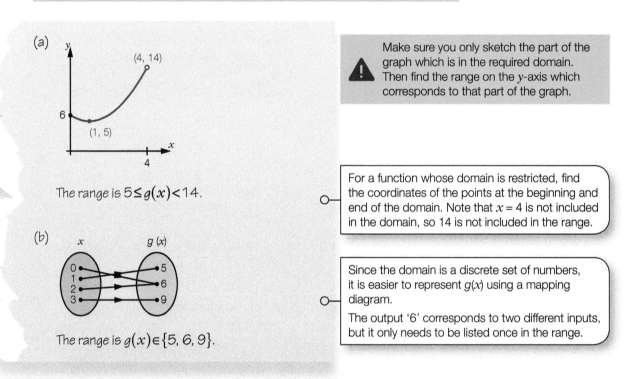

(a)

The range is $5 \leq g(x) < 14$.

⚠️ Make sure you only sketch the part of the graph which is in the required domain. Then find the range on the y-axis which corresponds to that part of the graph.

For a function whose domain is restricted, find the coordinates of the points at the beginning and end of the domain. Note that $x = 4$ is not included in the domain, so 14 is not included in the range.

(b)

The range is $g(x) \in \{5, 6, 9\}$.

Since the domain is a discrete set of numbers, it is easier to represent $g(x)$ using a mapping diagram.

The output '6' corresponds to two different inputs, but it only needs to be listed once in the range.

Practice questions 9.3

9. Write down the domain and range for the function whose graph is shown on the right.

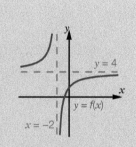

10. Find the range of the function $h(x) = x^2 - 4x + 7$.

11. The function f is defined by the mapping diagram shown.
   (a) Write down the domain and range of f.
   (b) Solve the equation $f(x) = 3$.

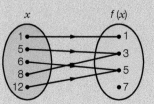

9.4 LINEAR MODELS

WORKED EXAMPLE 9.4

Sandra joins a gym that costs $30 per month plus $5 each time she uses the pool.

(a) Write down a formula for the amount, A, that Sandra spends at the gym in a month when she uses the pool n times.

(b) If Sandra spends $55 in a month, how many times did she use the pool?

(a) $A = 30 + 5n$

> If this answer is not clear, you could use the methods in Chapter 8 to find the equation of the line passing through (0, 30) and (1, 35).

(b) $55 = 30 + 5n$

$25 = 5n$

So $n = 5$.

> Use the information given to write down a linear equation and then solve for n.

Practice questions 9.4

12. A baby is born weighing 2.8 kg. He gains 150 g each week after birth.
   (a) Find a formula for the mass, m kg, of the baby n weeks after birth.
   (b) What is the mass of the baby after 4 weeks?
   (c) How long does it take for the baby to weigh 4 kg?

13. Alex has a choice of two mobile phone contracts. With Arithline he would pay £10 each month and each text would cost 2p. With Geomobile he would pay £12 each month and each text would cost 1p. How many texts would Alex need to send to make Geomobile the better deal?

14. Two taxi companies have different pricing structures. QuickCabs charges €1.20 per kilometre, plus a €2.40 callout charge. CityDrive has no callout charge, but the rate is €1.65 per kilometre. Let $C_1(d)$ and $C_2(d)$ be the costs of travelling d km with QuickCabs and CityDrive, respectively.
   (a) Write down expressions for C_1 and C_2.
   (b) Find the smallest number of whole kilometres for which QuickCabs is cheaper.

9.5 QUADRATIC FUNCTIONS AND MODELLING

WORKED EXAMPLE 9.5

Jamie estimates that her company will make a profit of p hundred thousand dollars if she sells n hundred cars. She models the profit as a quadratic function using the graph shown on the right.

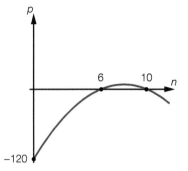

(a) The y-intercept of this graph is -120.
Explain what this means in the context of Jamie's company.

(b) Find the equation of the curve in the form $p = -2n^2 + an + b$ and hence estimate the profit when 700 cars are sold.

(c) Find the coordinates of the vertex of the curve and hence find the maximum profit estimated by the model.

(a) This means that if Jamie sold no cars her company would make a loss of $12 000 000.

> ⚠ Make sure you give your answer in context using appropriate units. A common error here would be to say 'a loss of $120'.

(b) When $n = 0$, $p = -120$, so:
$$-120 = -2 \times 0^2 + a \times 0 + b \Rightarrow b = -120$$
When $n = 6$, $p = 0$, so:
$$0 = -2 \times 6^2 + a \times 6 - 120$$
$$0 = 6a - 192 \Rightarrow a = 32$$
Therefore, $p = -2n^2 + 32n - 120$.

> ⚠ Substituting numbers into models to find the parameters is a very powerful technique. However, you could also have used the factorised form of the quadratic.

 You can use either (6, 0) or (10, 0) to find the value of a.

When $n = 7$,
$$p = -2 \times 7^2 + 32 \times 7 - 120 = 6$$
so a profit of $600 000 is made.

 700 cars corresponds to $n = 7$.

(c) The vertex occurs when $n = 8$, at which
$$p = -2 \times 8^2 + 32 \times 8 - 120 = 8$$
Estimated maximum profit is $800 000.

The n value of the vertex is half-way between the two roots.

Practice questions 9.5

15. (a) Factorise $ax - x^2$ and hence find the solutions to the equation $ax - x^2 = 0$.

The graph shows the path of a football after Melissa kicks it. The path can be modelled by the curve $y = ax - x^2$, where y is the height of the ball in metres above the ground and x is the horizontal distance in metres travelled by the ball.

(b) State the value of a.

(c) Find the maximum height reached by the football.

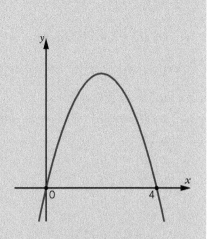

16. The height, h metres, that a model rocket reaches t seconds after launch is modelled by $h = kt - 4.9t^2$.

(a) Find the equation of the line of symmetry of the graph of h against t, giving your answer in terms of k.

(b) If the rocket can go at most $20\,\text{m}$ up into the air, find the value of k.

(c) If $k = 12$, find the two times at which the rocket is $5\,\text{m}$ above the ground.

17. The graph shown has equation $y = x^2 + bx + c$.

(a) Find the values of b and c.

(b) Find the coordinates of the vertex of the graph.

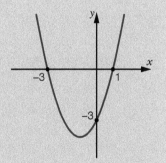

18. Which of the graphs correspond to the following functions?

(a) $y = x^2 + 4x$ (b) $y = x^2 - 2x + 2$ (c) $y = 3 - x^2$

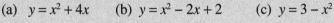

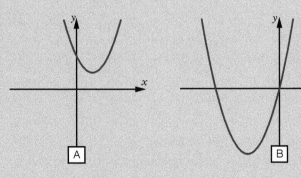

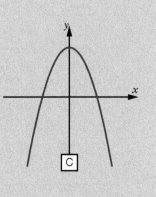

9.6 EXPONENTIAL FUNCTIONS AND MODELLING

WORKED EXAMPLE 9.6

The equation of the curve on the right is given by $y = k \times 2^x + 1$.

(a) Find the value of k.

(b) State the equation of the asymptote.

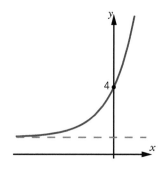

(a) When $x = 0, y = k \times 2^0 + 1 = k + 1 = 4$.

So $k = 3$.

Use the y-intercept $(0, 4)$ from the graph.

(b) $y = 1$

For any curve of the form $y = k \times a^x + c$, the horizontal asymptote is $y = c$.

If you forget this fact, you can sketch the graph on a GDC and trace along it to see what value y approaches.

Practice questions 9.6

19. The equation of the curve shown is given by $y = k \times 5^{-x} + c$.

(a) Find the values of k and c.

(b) If the domain of this function is $-2 < x < 2$, find the range of the function.

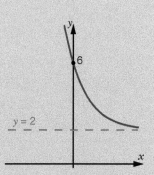

20. Jane fills a glass with hot water. The water cools towards the temperature of the room. The water's temperature, T degrees, at time t minutes is modelled by $T = 50 \times 4^{-t} + 16$.

(a) Find the initial temperature of the water.

(b) Find the room temperature.

(c) Find the temperature of the water after 2 minutes.

(d) How long will Jane have to wait for the temperature of the water to fall below 40 degrees?

21.

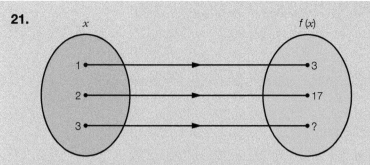

The diagram above is a mapping diagram for the function $f(x) = k \times 2^x + c$.

(a) Find the values of k and c.

(b) Find the value of $f(3)$.

22. The size of a population of bacteria, N thousand, d days after the start of an experiment can be modelled by the equation $N(d) = 3.2 + 1.2^d - 0.8d$.

(a) Use the model to complete the following table:

d (days)	0	2	4	6	8	10
N (thousands)						

(b) On graph paper, draw the graph of $N(d)$ for $0 \le d \le 10$. Use a scale of 5 mm for one unit.

(c) Use your graph to find:

(i)   the size of the population after 5 days

(ii) the minimum size of the population

(iii) the values of d for which the population is decreasing.

9.7 POLYNOMIAL FUNCTIONS AND MODELLING

WORKED EXAMPLE 9.7

A car's speed v, in km/h, varies with time t, in hours, according to the equation

$v = (25 - t^2)(t + 1)$ for $0 \leq t \leq 5$

(a) Find the maximum speed of the car.

(b) At what time does the car stop?

(c) Find the initial speed of the car, and one other time at which it is travelling at this speed.

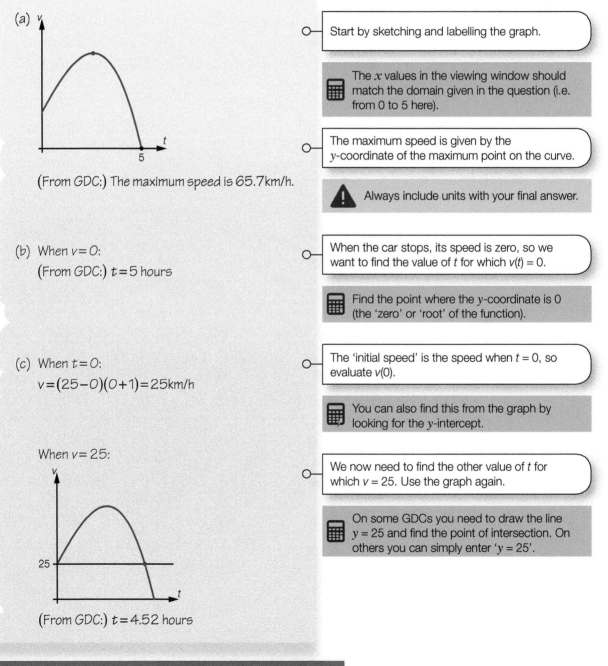

(a)

(From GDC:) The maximum speed is 65.7 km/h.

Start by sketching and labelling the graph.

The x values in the viewing window should match the domain given in the question (i.e. from 0 to 5 here).

The maximum speed is given by the y-coordinate of the maximum point on the curve.

⚠ Always include units with your final answer.

(b) When $v = 0$:

(From GDC:) $t = 5$ hours

When the car stops, its speed is zero, so we want to find the value of t for which $v(t) = 0$.

Find the point where the y-coordinate is 0 (the 'zero' or 'root' of the function).

(c) When $t = 0$:

$v = (25 - 0)(0 + 1) = 25$ km/h

The 'initial speed' is the speed when $t = 0$, so evaluate $v(0)$.

You can also find this from the graph by looking for the y-intercept.

When $v = 25$:

(From GDC:) $t = 4.52$ hours

We now need to find the other value of t for which $v = 25$. Use the graph again.

On some GDCs you need to draw the line $y = 25$ and find the point of intersection. On others you can simply enter '$y = 25$'.

Practice questions 9.7

23. A function is defined by $f(x) = 5 - 11x + 7x^2 - x^3$ for $0 \le x \le 5$.

    (a) Sketch the graph of $y = f(x)$.

    (b) Find the coordinates of the maximum and minimum points on the graph.

    (c) State the values of x for which $f(x)$ is increasing.

    (d) Find the values of x for which $f(x) = 4$.

24. A small company produces clocks. The cost (in £) of producing n clocks can be modelled by the equation $C(n) = 0.125n^2 + 2.5n + 200$. All the clocks produced are sold for £15 each.

    (a) Write down an equation for the revenue, £R, from selling n clocks.

    (b) The profit when n clocks are produced and sold is £$P(n)$. Show that $P(n) = 12.5n - 0.125n^2 - 200$.

    (c) Sketch the graph of $y = P(n)$ for $0 \le n \le 100$.

    (d) Describe the company's profit when 15 clocks are produced.

    (e) Find the smallest number of clocks the company needs to produce in order to make a profit.

    (f) How many clocks should the company produce in order to maximise the profit?

25. Consider the function $f(x) = x^4 - 8x^2 + 10$ defined for $-3 \le x \le 3$.

    (a) Sketch the graph of $y = f(x)$.

    (b) Find the zeros of the function.

    (c) Find the coordinates of the stationary points.

    (d) Find the positive value of x for which $f(x) = 15$.

9.8 RATIONAL FUNCTIONS AND THEIR GRAPHS

WORKED EXAMPLE 9.8

The graph $y = x^2 + kx^{-2}$ passes through the point $(1, 7)$.

(a) Find the value of k.

(b) State the equation of the vertical asymptote.

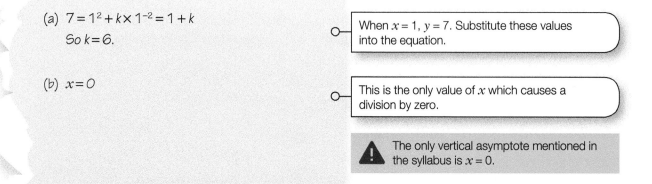

(a) $7 = 1^2 + k \times 1^{-2} = 1 + k$

So $k = 6$.

When $x = 1$, $y = 7$. Substitute these values into the equation.

(b) $x = 0$

This is the only value of x which causes a division by zero.

⚠ The only vertical asymptote mentioned in the syllabus is $x = 0$.

Practice questions 9.8

26. A graph has the equation $y = 3x^2 + \dfrac{a}{x}$ for $x > 0$. It passes through the point $(1, 8)$. Find the value of a.

27. (a) Find the domain and range of the function $f(x) = x + \dfrac{4}{x}$.

    (b) Use your calculator to find the solutions to the equation $f(x) = 5$.

28. Let $f(x) = x + 3x^{-1}$.

    (a) Sketch the graph of $f(x)$ using axes showing $-2 \le x \le 4$ and $-10 \le y \le 10$.

    (b) State the equation of the vertical asymptote of $f(x)$.

    (c) Find the range of $f(x)$ if the domain is $1 < x < 4$.

29. The graph has the equation $y = 3^x + \dfrac{k}{x}$.

    (a) Find the value of k.

    (b) State the equation of the vertical asymptote.

    (c) Solve the equation $3^x + \dfrac{k}{x} = 10$.

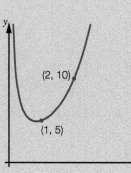

Mixed practice 9

1. Match these graphs to their equations in the table ($a, b, c, k, m > 0$ and $n > 1$).

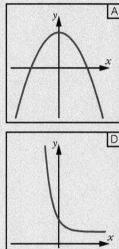 A

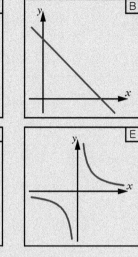 B

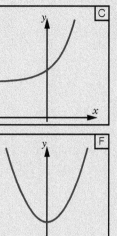 C

D

E

F

Equation	Graph
$y = a - x$	
$y = x^2 + m$	
$y = k + 5^{-x}$	
$y = c - x^2$	
$y = bx^{-1}$	
$y = 3 + n^x$	

2. A rectangle has sides $(x - 3)$ cm and $(x + 5)$ cm. The area of the rectangle is 68 cm². Find the value of x.

$(x - 3)$

$(x + 5)$

3. The function $h(x)$ is defined by $h(x) = x - \dfrac{2}{x^2}$.

    (a) Find the value of $h(3.2)$.

    (b) Solve the equation $h(x) = 5.6$.

4. The graph shows the function $f(x) = a \times 3^x + \dfrac{b}{x}, x > 0$.

    (a) Use the graph to find the values of a and b.

    (b) Solve the equation $f(x) = 7$.

    (c) Find the coordinates of the minimum point on the curve.

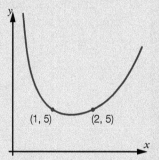

(1, 5)   (2, 5)

5. Butter is taken out of the fridge and left to warm up. The temperature of the butter, T°C, after m minutes is given by the equation $T = c - k \times 1.2^{-m}$. The initial temperature of the butter is 5°C, and after 5 minutes its temperature has increased to 15°C, as shown on the graph.

    (a) Find the values of k and c.

    (b) How long does it take for the butter to warm up to 20°C?

    (c) Find the equation of the asymptote of the graph. What does this value represent?

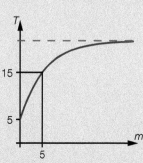

Going for the top 9

1. The graph of a quadratic function is shown in the diagram.

   Find the equation of the graph.

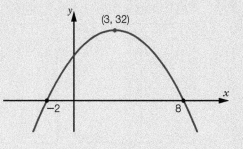

2. The diagram shows the graph of the function $f(x) = 3x^2 + x - 3$. The range of $f(x)$ is $1 \le f(x) < 77$. Find the domain of $f(x)$.

3. (a) Draw the curve $y = x + \dfrac{4}{x}$.

   (b) Use your calculator to find both solutions to the equation $x + \dfrac{4}{x} = 10$.

   (c) The equation $x + \dfrac{4}{x} = k$ has one solution. Find the two possible values of k.

4. The graph with equation $y = a + b(2^x)$ is shown on the right. Find the values of a and b.

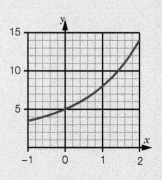

5. A function is defined by $g(x) = x^3 - ax + b$. The graph of $y = g(x)$ has gradient 3 at the point $(2, -2)$. Find the values of a and b.

10 DIFFERENTIATION

- The derivative of a function represents the gradient at a point on the curve, or the rate of change of the function.

- If $y = f(x)$, the derivative of the function is written as $f'(x)$ or $\dfrac{dy}{dx}$.

- The general rules of differentiation:
  - If $f(x) = ax^n$, then $f'(x) = nax^{n-1}$.
  - The derivative of a sum is the sum of the derivatives of the individual terms.
    So, if $f(x) = ax^n$ and $g(x) = bx^m$, then $\left(f(x) + g(x)\right)' = f'(x) + g'(x) = nax^{n-1} + mbx^{m-1}$.

- To find the equation of a tangent to a curve at a point, you need the coordinates (x_1, y_1) of the point and the gradient m at that point.
  - Use $y - y_1 = m(x - x_1)$ to find the equation of the tangent.

- The normal is the line perpendicular to the tangent at the point where it touches the curve.
  - To find the equation of the normal, use the fact that for perpendicular lines, $m_1 \times m_2 = -1$.

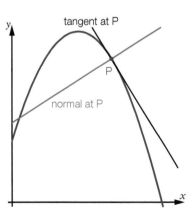

- If $f'(x) > 0$, the gradient is positive and the function is increasing.
  If $f'(x) < 0$, the gradient is negative and the function is decreasing.

- A stationary point occurs where $f'(x) = 0$. A stationary point can be a local minimum (where the curve changes from decreasing to increasing) or a local maximum (where the curve changes from increasing to decreasing).

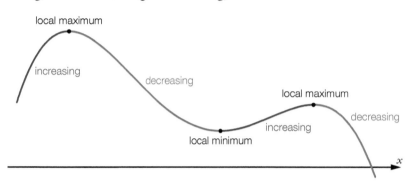

- To solve optimisation problems by finding a local maximum or minimum, find the solution to the equation $f'(x) = 0$.

⚠ EXAM TIPS AND COMMON ERRORS

- You may have met 'points of inflexion' on your course, but these will not be tested in the examination.

- Exam questions can use several different instructions which all mean 'find $\dfrac{dy}{dx}$' – for example, find $f'(x)$; differentiate with respect to x; find the gradient function; find the derivative of the function.

- If $y = c$ then $\dfrac{dy}{dx} = 0$.

- The rules for differentiation also work for negative powers. You will often need to use the fact that, for example, $\dfrac{1}{x^2} = x^{-2}$. Be very careful if there are coefficients, e.g. $\dfrac{1}{3x^2} = \dfrac{1}{3}x^{-2}$.

- Your GDC cannot differentiate a function for you, but it can draw the curve, find the gradient of a function at any point, and find maximum and minimum points. Make sure you know how to do these tasks using your GDC.

- When setting up equations, be very clear whether you have information about $f(x)$ or $f'(x)$.

- Not all functions have x as the variable. Do not get confused if other letters are used instead.

- Make sure that you answer the question asked. If x values are requested, give only x values. If coordinates are requested, give both x and y values.

- It can be very useful to sketch the graph of the function.

10.1 DIFFERENTIATION

WORKED EXAMPLE 10.1

Let $f(x) = 3x^2 + \dfrac{1}{10x^2} - 1$.

(a) Find $f'(x)$.

(b) Evaluate $f'(1)$ and explain what your answer represents.

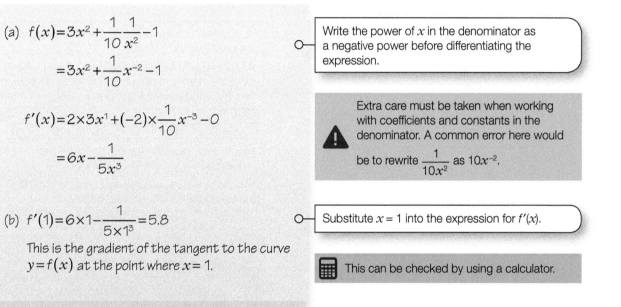

(a) $f(x) = 3x^2 + \dfrac{1}{10}\dfrac{1}{x^2} - 1$

$= 3x^2 + \dfrac{1}{10}x^{-2} - 1$

$f'(x) = 2 \times 3x^1 + (-2) \times \dfrac{1}{10}x^{-3} - 0$

$= 6x - \dfrac{1}{5x^3}$

(b) $f'(1) = 6 \times 1 - \dfrac{1}{5 \times 1^3} = 5.8$

This is the gradient of the tangent to the curve $y = f(x)$ at the point where $x = 1$.

Write the power of x in the denominator as a negative power before differentiating the expression.

Extra care must be taken when working with coefficients and constants in the denominator. A common error here would be to rewrite $\dfrac{1}{10x^2}$ as $10x^{-2}$.

Substitute $x = 1$ into the expression for $f'(x)$.

This can be checked by using a calculator.

Practice questions 10.1

1. A curve has equation $f(x) = 3x^2 + 10x - 5$.
   (a) Find $f'(x)$.
   (b) Find the coordinates of the point on the curve $y = f(x)$ where the gradient is 31.

2. The temperature of a kettle, $T°C$, is given by $26 + \dfrac{t^2}{50}$, where t is the time in seconds since the kettle was turned on.
   (a) Find $\dfrac{dT}{dt}$.
   (b) Evaluate $\dfrac{dT}{dt}$ one minute after the kettle has been turned on and explain what your answer means in the context of the boiling kettle.

10.2 EQUATIONS OF THE TANGENT AND NORMAL

WORKED EXAMPLE 10.2

A curve has equation $y = 3x^2 - 5x + 2$.

(a) Find the equation of the normal to the curve at $x = 2$.

(b) Find the coordinates of the point where the tangent to the curve is parallel to the line $y + x = 5$.

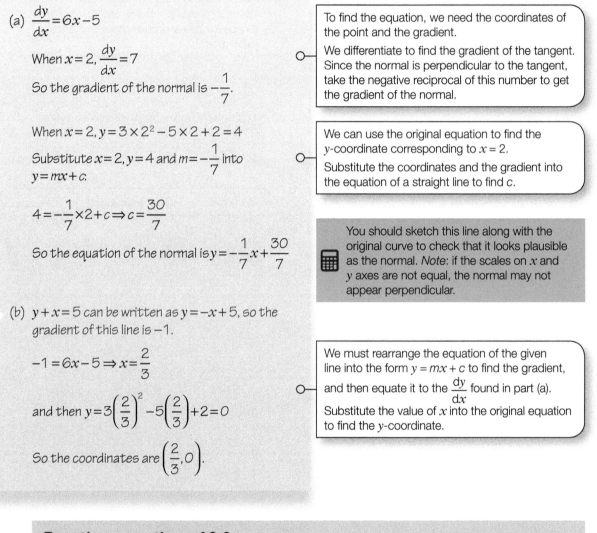

(a) $\dfrac{dy}{dx} = 6x - 5$

> To find the equation, we need the coordinates of the point and the gradient.

When $x = 2$, $\dfrac{dy}{dx} = 7$

So the gradient of the normal is $-\dfrac{1}{7}$.

> We differentiate to find the gradient of the tangent. Since the normal is perpendicular to the tangent, take the negative reciprocal of this number to get the gradient of the normal.

When $x = 2$, $y = 3 \times 2^2 - 5 \times 2 + 2 = 4$

Substitute $x = 2$, $y = 4$ and $m = -\dfrac{1}{7}$ into $y = mx + c$.

> We can use the original equation to find the y-coordinate corresponding to $x = 2$.
>
> Substitute the coordinates and the gradient into the equation of a straight line to find c.

$4 = -\dfrac{1}{7} \times 2 + c \Rightarrow c = \dfrac{30}{7}$

So the equation of the normal is $y = -\dfrac{1}{7}x + \dfrac{30}{7}$

> You should sketch this line along with the original curve to check that it looks plausible as the normal. *Note*: if the scales on x and y axes are not equal, the normal may not appear perpendicular.

(b) $y + x = 5$ can be written as $y = -x + 5$, so the gradient of this line is -1.

$-1 = 6x - 5 \Rightarrow x = \dfrac{2}{3}$

and then $y = 3\left(\dfrac{2}{3}\right)^2 - 5\left(\dfrac{2}{3}\right) + 2 = 0$

> We must rearrange the equation of the given line into the form $y = mx + c$ to find the gradient, and then equate it to the $\dfrac{dy}{dx}$ found in part (a).
>
> Substitute the value of x into the original equation to find the y-coordinate.

So the coordinates are $\left(\dfrac{2}{3}, 0\right)$.

Practice questions 10.2

3. A curve has equation $y = 1 - \dfrac{6}{x}$.

    (a) Find the equation of the tangent to the curve at $x = 2$.

    (b) Find the coordinates of the points on the curve where the gradient is $\dfrac{2}{3}$.

4. If $y = x^2 + 5x$, find the equation of the normal with gradient 1.

10.3 STATIONARY POINTS AND OPTIMISATION

WORKED EXAMPLE 10.3

The annual profit, P thousands of euros, made when a firm sells x hundreds of handbags is given by $P = 10x - x^2 - 10$.

(a) What value does P take when $x = 0$? Explain what your answer means in the context of the firm.

(b) Find the value of x for which $\dfrac{\mathrm{d}P}{\mathrm{d}x} = 0$.

(c) What is the maximum profit the firm can make? How many handbags must it sell to make this profit?

(a) When $x = 0$, $P = -10$.

This means that when no bags are sold, the firm makes a loss of €10 000.

○— Substitute $x = 0$ into the expression for P.

(b) $\dfrac{\mathrm{d}P}{\mathrm{d}x} = 10 - 2x = 0$ when $x = 5$

(c)
(5, 15)

Looking at the graph, the stationary point gives the maximum profit.

⚠ A quick sketch graph may earn you some method marks even if you don't complete the answer.

The maximum point occurs when $x = 5$ and $P = 15$. This means that the firm makes a profit of €15 000 when 500 bags are sold.

○— Use a calculator to get the coordinates of the stationary point, or use the answer from part (b).

Practice questions 10.3

5. For the function $f(x) = x + x^2 - 10$, find the value of x for which $f'(x) = 0$ and state what this means in the context of the graph $y = f(x)$.

6. (a) Sketch the graph of $y = x^3 - 4x + 4$.
   (b) Find the coordinates of the local minimum point.
   (c) State the values of x for which the graph is decreasing.

7. Let $f(x) = x^3 - 12x + 2$.
   (a) Find the values of x for which $f(x) = 0$.
   (b) Find the values of x for which $f'(x) = 0$.
   (c) Find the coordinates of the local maximum point on the graph $y = f(x)$.
   (d) Find the coordinates of the local minimum point on the graph $y = f(x)$.

8. The energy E, in electronvolts, of a molecule with a bond length L, in angstroms, is given by:
$$E = 12L + \frac{20}{L}, \quad L > 0$$
   (a) Sketch the graph of E against L.
   (b) Find, by differentiating, the minimum energy of the molecule.

9. (a) Sketch the graph of $y = 9 - x^2$ for $-3 \le x \le 3$.
   (b) State the equation of the line of symmetry of the curve.

   A rectangle has one side on the x-axis and lies beneath the curve drawn in part (a), touching the curve at the point with x-coordinate p, where $p > 0$.
   (c) Show that the area of the rectangle is $18p - 2p^3$.
   (d) Find the maximum area of the rectangle.

10. An oil barrel is in the shape of a closed cylinder with radius r m and height h m. It has a surface area of 2π m^2.
    (a) Show that $h = \frac{1}{r} - r$.
    (b) Find the maximum volume of the barrel.
    (c) 80 m^3 of oil is to be stored in such barrels. What is the smallest number of barrels required?

11. A piece of wire of length 100 cm is cut into two pieces. One piece is made into a circle of radius r cm. The other is made into a square of side x cm.
    (a) Show that $x = 25 - \frac{\pi}{2}r$.
    (b) Find the maximum total area of the two shapes.

Mixed practice 10

1. Consider the function $f(x) = x^2 + \dfrac{3}{x}$.

   (a) Find $f'(x)$.

   (b) Find the gradient of the tangent at the point with coordinates $(3, 10)$.

2. Find the set of values for which the function $f(x) = 3x^2 + 4x + 7$ is decreasing.

    Exam questions often ask for the values of x for which $f(x)$ is increasing or decreasing – the y value doesn't matter.

3. Find the coordinates of the point on the curve $y = x^2 - 6x + 5$ where the gradient of the tangent is 4.

4. If $y = x^3 - 6x$, find the tangents which are parallel to the line $y = 21x + 4$.

5. The tangent to the curve $y = ax^2 + 4x + b$ at the point $x = 2$ has the equation $y = 24x - 23$. Find the values of a and b.

6. The height of a shrub, h cm, at a time t days after it is planted is modelled by $h = t^2 + t^3 + 12$.

   (a) What was the height of the shrub when it was initially planted?

   (b) What is the height of the shrub after 3 days?

   (c) What is the rate of change of height after 3 days?

7. Consider the function $f(x) = 4x^4 - \dfrac{1}{2x} + 5$.

   (a) Find $f(2)$.

   (b) Find $f'(2)$.

   (c) Find the equation of the normal to the curve $y = f(x)$ at $x = 2$.

8. Find the coordinates of the points on the graph $y = x^3 - 12x + 4$ where the tangent is parallel to the x-axis.

9. A cuboid has dimensions x metres by x metres by y metres. It has a surface area of $100\,\mathrm{m}^2$.

   (a) Show that $y = \dfrac{25}{x} - \dfrac{x}{2}$.

   (b) Show that the volume is $25x - \dfrac{x^3}{2}$.

   (c) Find the maximum volume of the cuboid.

10. Consider the function $f(x) = 2x^3 - 9x^2 + 12x + 5$.

    (a) Write down $f'(x)$.

    (b) Find all the solutions to $f'(x) = 0$.

    (c) Hence find the coordinates of the stationary points on the curve $y = f(x)$.

    (d) Sketch the graph of $y = f(x)$.

    (e) Write down the intervals in which $f(x)$ is increasing.

11. Consider the function $f(x) = ax + \dfrac{1}{2x} + 5$.

    (a) Write down $f(1)$ in terms of a.

    (b) Write down $f'(x)$.

    (c) The tangent to the curve $y = f(x)$ at $x = 1$ has gradient $\dfrac{7}{2}$. Find the value of a.

    N is the normal to the curve at $x = 1$.

    (d) (i) Show that the equation of N can be written as $14y + 4x = 137$.

        (ii) Find the coordinates of the point where the normal found in part (d)(i) meets the curve again.

    (e) Sketch the curve $y = f(x)$ for $0 < x \le 4$ and $0 \le y \le 20$.

    (f) Use your GDC to find the coordinates of the minimum point on the curve $y = f(x)$.

    (g) Find the interval within $0 < x \le 4$ in which $f(x)$ is decreasing.

Going for the top 10

1. The curve $y = ax^2 + bx + 4$ has a maximum point at (4, 8). Find the values of a and b.

2. The equation of the tangent to the curve $y = ax^3 + 3x + b$ at $x = 1$ is given by $y = 15x - 2$. Find the values of a and b.

3. Jane throws a ball from 1 m above the ground to Hilary, who catches it 1 m above the ground. The equation of the path of the ball is given by $y = 4x - 0.8x^2$, where x is the horizontal distance and y is the height of the ball above the ground, both measured in metres.

    (a) How far apart are Jane and Hilary standing?

    (b) What is the maximum height that the ball reaches?

11 EXAMINATION SUPPORT

COMMON ERRORS

There are several very common errors which you need to be aware of.
- Making up rules which don't exist, such as:

    - $(x + y)^2 = x^2 + y^2$
      [*Note*: The correct expansion is $x^2 + 2xy + y^2$.]

- Algebraic errors, especially involving minus signs and brackets, such as:

    - $3 - (1 - 2x) = 3 - 1 - 2x$
      [*Note*: The correct expansion is $3 - 1 + 2x$.]

    - $(5x)^3 = 5x^3$
      [*Note*: The correct expansion is $125x^3$.]

- Arithmetic errors, especially involving fractions, such as:

    - $3 \times \dfrac{2}{5} = \dfrac{6}{15}$
      [*Note*: The correct answer is $\dfrac{6}{5}$.]

- Not thinking about the order of operations when inputting calculations into a calculator; for example:

    - 3×5^2 [Answer: 75] is not the same as $(3 \times 5)^2$ [Answer: 225]

    - -3^2 [Answer: −9] is not the same as $(-3)^2$ [Answer: 9]

    - 2^{3x} must be entered as '2^(3 x)' [not '2^3×x']

Spot the common errors

Find the errors in the solutions below.

1. Find the fifth term of a geometric sequence with first term 3 and common ratio 2.

Solution: $u_5 = u_1 \times r^4$
$$= 3 \times 2^4$$
$$= 6^4 = 1296$$

2. An arithmetic sequence has first term 5 and common difference −3.
Find the value of n for which $S_n = -775$.

Solution:
$$S_n = \frac{n}{2}(2u_1 + (n-1)d)$$

$$-775 = \frac{n}{2}(2 \times 5 + (n-1)(-3))$$

$$-1550 = n(10 - 3n - 3)$$

$$-1550 = 7n - 3n^2$$

$$3n^2 - 7n - 1550 = 0$$

$$n = 24 \text{ (from GDC)}$$

3. Sketch the graph of $y = 5 + 2^{2x}$.

   Solution:

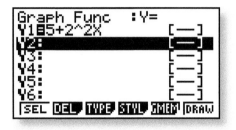 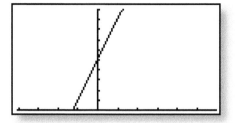

4. Given that $y = 2x - \dfrac{1}{3x}$, find $\dfrac{dy}{dx}$.

   Solution: $y = 2x - 3x^{-1}$

   $$\frac{dy}{dx} = 2 + 3x^{-2}$$

5. Solve the equation $(x - 3)^2 = 2x + 1$.

   Solution: $x^2 - 9 = 2x + 1$

   $x^2 - 2x - 10 = 0$

   $x = 4.32 \text{ or } -2.32$

6. Perform the following calculations using a GDC.

   (a) Find the value of $4 + 3x^2$ when $x = -5$.

   Solution:

   $4 + 3 \times -5^2 = -71$

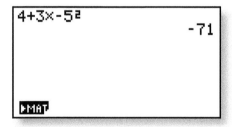

   (b) $4 \times 3^{1.02 + 3.07} =$

   Solution:

   15.3 (3 SF)

(c) $\sqrt{4.2 - 1.7} =$

Solution:

```
√4.2-1.7
              0.3493901532




▶MAT
```

0.349 (3 SF)

HOW TO CHECK YOUR ANSWERS

What you need to know

Checking questions by reading through your previous working is usually not very effective. You need to try more subtle methods such as:

- using your calculator to check a solution you obtained algebraically
- estimating the answer
- substituting numbers into algebraic expressions.

It is vital that you know how to use your calculator to check work. It often requires a little imagination.

Example 1: Algebraic manipulation

Suppose you were asked to expand $(1 + 2x)^2$ and you got $1 + 4x + 2x^2$.

Substituting $x = 3$ into the original expression gives $7^2 = 49$. Substituting $x = 3$ into your answer gives 31, so something has gone wrong.

 This method (substitution) can be used to check each line of working to identify where the mistake occurred.

Example 2: Differentiation

Suppose you were asked to differentiate $3x^2$ and you said that the answer was $6x$.

If this is the derivative, then the gradient at $x = 3$ would be $6 \times 3 = 18$. According to the differentiation function on the calculator, the gradient at $x = 3$ is 18, so your answer is plausible.

 Just because these numbers agree doesn't mean the answer is correct – it could be a coincidence. However, it should give you the confidence to move on and check another question!

 If you are finding the equation of a tangent, you should also plot it and the original curve on the same graph to make sure it looks like a tangent.

Example 3: Problems involving parameters

Many questions try to eliminate the option of using a calculator by putting an additional unknown into the question. For example, suppose a question asked you to find the range of the function $f(x) = a + 2^{-x}$, giving your answer in terms of a.

If you thought the answer was $f(x) > a$, then you could check this by sketching the graph with $a = 3$. The graph has a horizontal asymptote at $y = 3$, which is consistent with the range being $f(x) > a$.

THINGS YOU NEED TO KNOW HOW TO DO ON YOUR CALCULATOR

CASIO CALCULATOR

Note: These instructions were written based on the calculator model fx-9860G SD and may not be applicable to other models. If in doubt, refer to your calculator's manual.

Skill	On a Casio calculator	
Store numbers as variables	In the RUN menu use the → button and then key in a letter.	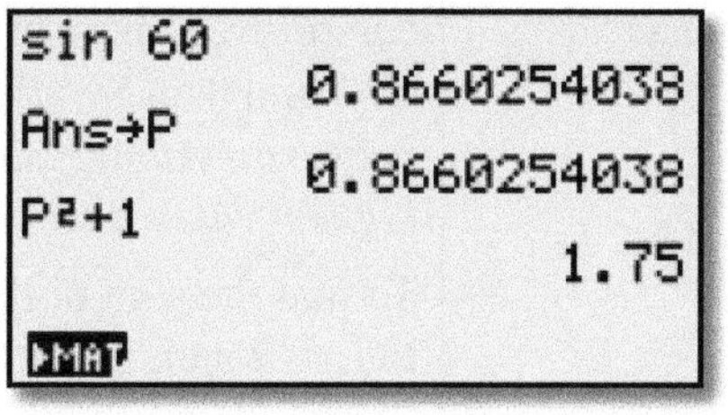 sin 60 0.8660254038 Ans→P 0.8660254038 P²+1 1.75 ▶MAT
Solve equations graphically	In the GRAPH menu input one equation into Y1 and the other into Y2. Go to the G-Solv menu (F5), and use the ISCT (F5) function to find the intersection. If there is more than one intersection, press across (F6) to move the cursor to the next intersection point.	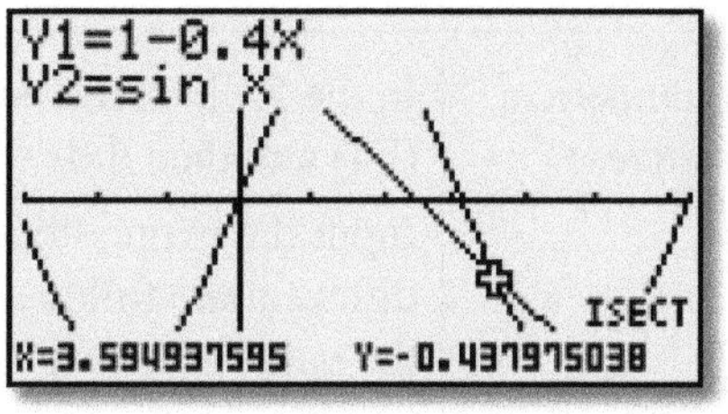 Y1=1−0.4X Y2=sin X ISECT X=3.594937595 Y=−0.437975038
Solve equations numerically	In the RUN menu press OPTN, CALC (F4) and then SolveN (F5). Put in the equation you want to solve.	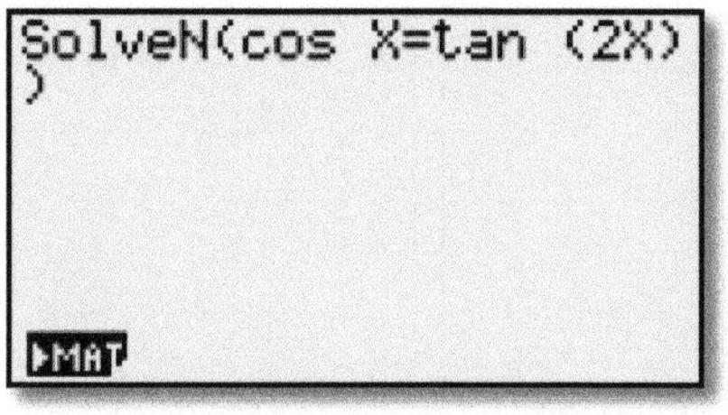  SolveN(cos X=tan (2X)) ▶MAT Ans 1 [−7.853] 2 −5.908 3 −4.712 4 −3.516 5 −1.57 −7.853981634

Skill	On a Casio calculator
Solve linear simultaneous equations	In the EQUA menu press F1 for simultaneous equations. Rearrange the equations into the form $ax + by + cz = d$ and input all the coefficients. anX+bnY+CnZ=dn a | b | c | d 1 | 1 | 2 | 3 | 4 2 | 1 | 3 | 5 | 7 3 | 0 | 1 | -1 | 0 1 [SOLV] [DEL] [CLR] [EDIT]
Put sequences into lists	Go to the STAT menu. With the cursor over List 1 press OPTN, List (F1) and then Seq (F5). The syntax is Seq(*expression*, X, *lowest value*, *highest value*, *increment*). To find the sum of the sequence, go to List 2 and, using the same menu as before, go across to get Cuml and then List 1. List 1 | List 2 | List 3 | List 4 SUB 1 | 2 | 2 2 | 5 | 7 3 | 8 | 15 4 | 11 | 26 Cuml List 1
Find numerical derivatives	In the RUN menu press OPTN, CALC (F4) and then d/dx (F2). Input the expression you want to differentiate followed by a comma and the value at which you want to evaluate the derivative. If you want to sketch a derivative you can use this expression in a graph too. d/dx(sin (3X),π) -3 ▶MAT Graph Func :Y= Y1◨X^3-2X²+X [—] Y2◨d/dx(Y1,X) [—] Y3: [—] Y4: [—] Y5: [—] Y6: [—] [SEL] [DEL] [TYPE] [STYL] [GMEM] [DRAW]
Find maximum and minimum points on a graph	In the GRAPH menu, plot the graph and press G-Solv (F5). Then press Max (F2) or Min (F3). Y1=X^3-2X²+X MAX X=0.3333333319 Y=0.1481481481

Skill	On a Casio calculator	
| Find sample statistics | In the STAT menu enter the data in List 1 and, if required, the frequencies in List 2. Press CALC (F2). Use SET (F6) to make sure that the 1-Var XList is List 1 and that 1-Var Freq is either 1 or List 2, as appropriate. Then exit and press 1-Var (F1). Scrolling down shows the median and quartiles. | ```
1-Variable
x̄     =3.9090909
Σx    =172
Σx²   =860
σx    =2.06505758
sx    =2.08893187
n     =44          ↓
``` |
| Find the product–moment correlation coefficient and the equation of the regression line | In the STAT menu, enter the $x$ values into List 1 and the $y$ values into List 2. Then go to CALC (F2), REG (F3), X (F1), a$x$+b (F1).<br><br>The resulting display shows the coefficients ($a$ and $b$) in the equation of the regression line ($y = ax + b$) and the correlation coefficient ($r$). | ```
LinearReg(ax+b)
   a =0.33333333
   b =1
   r =0.87545608
   r²=0.76642335
  MSe=1.33333333
y=ax+b
              COPY
``` |
| Use inverse normal functions | To find the boundaries of a region with a specified probability, go to the STAT menu, then DIST (F5), NORM (F1) and InvN (F3). Input the data as a variable.<br><br>Depending on the information you have, you can use different 'tails': for P($X < x$) use the left tail, for P($X > x$) use the right tail, and for P($-x < X < x$) use the central tail.<br><br>Input the mean and standard deviation. Use $\mu = 0$ and $\sigma = 1$ if you do not know the mean or standard deviation and want to find a Z-score. | ```
Inverse Normal
Data   :Variable
Tail   :Left
Area   :0.95
σ      :1
μ      :0
Save Res:None      ↓
``` |
```

Skill	On a Casio calculator
Perform a chi-squared test on a contingency table	Press CALC, TEST (F3), CHI (F3). You may then need to select 2WAY (F2). Then press >MAT (F2), DIM (F3) to enter the observed frequencies. Press EXIT twice to return to the chi-squared screen, and select CALC (F1).

The calculator will display the chi-squared value, the p-value and the number of degrees of freedom (df). The expected frequencies are saved in matrix B, and you can view them by pressing Mat (F1) and then DIM (F3) in the main (RUN) menu.

Note that the calculator does not check whether some rows or columns need to be combined. |

x^2 Test
Observed:Mat A
Expected:Mat B
Save Res:None
Execute

Mat ▶MAT

Matrix
Dimension m×n
  m :3
  n :4
Mat F   :None
DEL DEL·A DIM

x^2 Test
Observed:Mat A
Expected:Mat B
Save Res:None
Execute

CALC   DRAW

x^2 Test
  x^2=13.4580758
  p =0.0363117
  df=6

▶MAT

TEXAS CALCULATOR

Note: These instructions were written based on the calculator model TI-84 Plus Silver Edition and may not be applicable to other models. If in doubt, refer to your calculator's manual.

Skill	On a Texas calculator	

Store numbers as variables	In the RUN menu, use the STO▶ button and then key in a letter.	sin(60)
		        .8660254038
		Ans→P
		        .8660254038
		P²+1
		             1.75

Solve equations graphically	In the Y= menu, input one equation into Y1 and the other into Y2. Then press the GRAPH button. You may need to use the WINDOW or ZOOM functions to find an appropriate scale. To look for intersections, press CALC (2nd, F4) then intersect (F5). You must select the two graphs you want to intersect and move the cursor close to the intersection point you are interested in.	Intersection X=3.5949376 Y=-.437975
Solve equations numerically	In the MATH menu press Solve (0). You must rearrange your equation into the form . . . = 0. Input this and press Solve (ALPHA, ENTER) when the cursor is above the X value. To find other values, change the bounds within which you want the calculator to search. For polynomial equations, you can find all solutions by using the solver in the PolySmlt 2 APP (which is recommended by the IB).	cos(X)-tan(2X)=0 ■X=■37473443270… bound=(-1 E99,1… ■left-rt=0

Skill	On a Texas calculator
Solve linear simultaneous equations	In the PolySmlt APP select 'SimultEqnSolver' (2). You can change the number of equations and the number of unknowns. Rearrange the equations into the form $ax + by + cz = d$ and input all the coefficients. If the solution is not unique, a parametric representation of the solution will be given.
Put sequences into lists	Press LIST (2nd, STAT) and move across to OPS. Option 5 is seq, an operation which puts a sequence into a list. The syntax is seq(*rule*, X, *lower limit, upper limit, step*). You can store this sequence in a list using the STO▶ button. To look at the cumulative sum of your sequence, use the cumSum function from the same menu.
Find numerical derivatives	In the MATH menu, option 8 is the numerical derivative, nDeriv. The syntax is nDeriv(*function*, X, *value of interest*). If you want to sketch the derivative function, you can graph Y1 = nDeriv(*function*, X, X).
Find maximum and minimum points on a graph	When viewing a graph in the CALC menu (2nd, F4), press minimum (3) or maximum (4). Use the cursor to describe the left and right sides of the region you want to look in and then click the cursor close to the stationary point.

Skill	On a Texas calculator
Find sample statistics	In the STAT menu, use the edit function to enter the data in List 1 and, if required, the frequencies in List 2. Press STAT and CALC, then 1-Var Stats (1) as appropriate. Give the name of the list which holds the data and, if required, the list which holds the frequencies. Scrolling down shows the median and quartiles. **1-Var Stats** x̄=9.868421053 Σx=375 Σx²=5161 Sx=6.282412399 σx=6.199197964 ↓n=38
Find the product– moment correlation coefficient and the equation of the regression line	If you need to find the correlation coefficient, first go to the CATALOG and select DiagnosticOn. In the STAT menu, use the EDIT function to enter x values into list L1 and y values into list L2. Press STAT and CALC then LinReg(ax+b) (4). Make sure the correct lists are being used. You can choose to save the equation of the regression line to be plotted on a graph; to do so, press VARS and then select Y-Vars, Function, Y1. The resulting screen shows the coefficients (a and b) in the equation of the regression line ($y = ax + b$) and the correlation coefficient (r). **LinReg** y=ax+b a=.2857142857 b=2.333333333 r²=.0669642857 r=.2587745848
Use inverse normal functions	If you know the probability of an event being below a particular point of a normal distribution, you can find the value of that point. In the DISTR menu (2nd, VARS), use the invNorm function with the syntax invNorm(*probability*, μ, σ). Use μ = 0 and σ = 1 if you do not know the mean or standard deviation and want to find a Z-score. invNorm(0.6,0,1) .2533471011

Skill	On a Texas calculator
Perform a chi-squared test on a contingency table	First, enter the observed frequencies: press MATRIX (2nd x^{-1}), then EDIT, then [A] (1). You need to set the dimensions and then enter the frequencies.

Go to the STAT menu and select TESTS, then χ^2-Test (C). Make sure the observed matrix is set to [A], then select Calculate. The calculator will display the chi-squared value, the p-value and the number of degrees of freedom (df). The expected frequencies are saved in matrix B, and you can view them by going back to the matrix menu.

Note that the calculator does not check whether some rows or columns need to be combined. |

Calculator screens:

```
MATRIX[A]  3 ×3
[ 14      22      31  ]
[ 31      42      17  ]
[ 23      31      12  ]

3,3=12
```

```
χ²-Test
Observed:[A]
Expected:[B]
Calculate Draw
```

```
χ²-Test
χ²=18.39287693
p=.0010339178
df=4
```

13 WORKED SOLUTIONS

1 WORKING WITH NUMBERS

Mixed practice 1

1.
(a) In decimal form $y = 1.46 \times 10^{-3}$ is 0.00146. The fifth decimal place is 6, so round up to 0.0015.

(b) $xy = (1.23 \times 10^5) \times (1.46 \times 10^{-3}) = 179.58$

(c) $\dfrac{y}{x} = \dfrac{1.46 \times 10^{-3}}{1.23 \times 10^5} = 1.19 \times 10^{-8}$

2.
(a) In decimal form the numbers are: $3.14 \times 10^2 = 314$, $100\pi = 314.159\ldots$, $\dfrac{2200}{7} = 314.285\ldots$, $\sqrt{100000} = 316.227\ldots$, 310. The largest is $\sqrt{100000}$.

(b)
(i) The integers are 3.14×10^2, 310.

(ii) The rational numbers are 3.14×10^2, $\dfrac{2200}{7}$, 310.

(c) The numbers are all equal to 300 correct to 1 SF.

3.
(a) $3000\,\text{m} \times 5000\,\text{m} = 15\,000\,000\,\text{m}^2 = 1.5 \times 10^7\,\text{m}^2$

(b) $1.5 \times 10^7 \div 3.4 = 4\,411\,764.7\ldots \approx 4\,412\,000$ to the nearest thousand

4. To take into account the 5% commission, all amounts need to be multiplied by 0.95.

(a) $10\,000 \times 0.95 \div 103 = 92.23$ dollars

(b) $500 \times 0.95 \times 103 = 48\,925$ yen

5.
(a) 1.25987×10^2

(b) The third significant figure from the left is 5, so round up to 130.

(c) $\dfrac{130 - 125.987}{125.987} \times 100\% = 3.185\ldots\% = 3.19\%$

6. Offer 1 converts 1 pound to 1.26 euros. With 5% commission, Offer 2 converts 1 pound to $1.30 \times 0.95 = 1.235$ euros. So Offer 1 provides the better deal.

7. Note that $\tan 45° = 1$ and $\tan 60° = \sqrt{3}$.

Number	$\mathbb{N}$	$\mathbb{Z}$	$\mathbb{Q}$	$\mathbb{R}$
−5	✗	✓	✓	✓
0	✓	✓	✓	✓
$\tan 45°$	✓	✓	✓	✓
$\tan 60°$	✗	✗	✗	✓

Number	$\mathbb{N}$	$\mathbb{Z}$	$\mathbb{Q}$	$\mathbb{R}$
9.9×10^{24}	✓	✓	✓	✓
1×10^{-2}	✗	✗	✓	✓
π	✗	✗	✗	✓

8.
(a) $V = \dfrac{4}{3}\pi(6700)^3 = 1.26 \times 10^{12}\,\text{km}^3$

(b) $1\,\text{km} = 1000\,\text{m} = 100\,000\,\text{cm}$, so $r = 670\,000\,000\,\text{cm} = 6.7 \times 10^8\,\text{cm}$

$V = \dfrac{4}{3}\pi(6.7 \times 10^8)^3 = 1.26 \times 10^{27}\,\text{cm}^3$

(c) $1.26 \times 10^{27}\,\text{cm}^3 \times 6.7\,\text{g/cm}^3 = 8.44 \times 10^{27}\,\text{g}$

Going for the top 1

1.
(a) $15 \le x < 25$

(b) $3 \times 15 - 7 = 38$

(c) The possible values of y are $1.55 \le y < 1.65$, so:

- the smallest possible value of $\dfrac{x}{y}$ is $\dfrac{15}{1.65} = 9.0909\ldots$

- the largest possible value of $\dfrac{x}{y}$ is $\dfrac{25}{1.55} = 16.1290\ldots$

The corresponding percentage errors are:

- $\left|\dfrac{12.5 - 9.0909\ldots}{9.0909\ldots}\right| \times 100\% = 37.5\%$

- $\left|\dfrac{12.5 - 16.1290\ldots}{16.1290\ldots}\right| \times 100\% = 22.5\%$

So the largest percentage error is 37.5%.

2.
(a) 1 USD = 0.66 GBP, so 1 GBP = $1 \div 0.66$ USD = 1.52 USD

(b) 1 USD = 0.78 EUR, so 1 EUR = $1 \div 0.78$ USD = 1.282 USD

1 USD = 102.48 JPY, so 1.282 USD = 1.282×102.48 JPY = 131.38 JPY

(c) Since the rate is the same when converting from USD as when converting back to USD, she only loses money on commission, which is paid 6 times.

So at the end she has $1000 \times (0.95)^6 = 735$ USD, to the nearest USD.

2 SEQUENCES AND SERIES

Mixed practice 2

1. (a) $u_1 + 2d = 5$, $u_1 + 6d = 11$

   (b) Using the GDC (or by elimination, i.e. subtracting the two equations), $d = 1.5$ and $u_1 = 2$

   (c) $S_{100} = \dfrac{100}{2}(2 \times 2 + 99 \times 1.5) = 7625$

2. We know that $u_1 = 1$, $u_n = 19$ and $S_n = 300$. So

   $S_n = \dfrac{n}{2}(u_1 + u_n)$

   $\Rightarrow 300 = \dfrac{n}{2}(1 + 19)$

   $\Rightarrow 300 = n \times 10$

   $\Rightarrow n = 30$

3. $u_4 = 17 \Rightarrow a + 3d = 17 \cdots (1)$

   $S_{20} = 990$

   $\Rightarrow \dfrac{20}{2}(2a + 19d) = 990$

   $\Rightarrow 2a + 19d = 99 \cdots (2)$

   Solving (1) and (2) simultaneously with the GDC gives $a = 2$, $d = 5$.

4. The teacher's annual salary over the years forms a geometric sequence with $u_1 = 25000$ and $r = 1.03$.

   (a) $u_{10} = 25000 \times 1.03^9 = \$32\,619.33$

   (b) $S_{35} = \dfrac{25000 \times (1.03^{35} - 1)}{1.03 - 1} = \$1\,511\,552$

   (c) $u_n = 25000 \times 1.03^{n-1} > 35\,000$

   Looking at the table on the GDC, the first n for which this holds is $n = 13$.

   (d) $S_n \geq 1\,000\,000 \Rightarrow \dfrac{25000 \times (1.03^n - 1)}{1.03 - 1} \geq 1\,000\,000$

   Looking at the table on the GDC, the first n for which this holds is $n = 27$.

5. The natural numbers from 1 to 100 form an arithmetic sequence with $u_1 = 1$, $n = 100$ and $u_{100} = 100$.

   $S_n = \dfrac{n}{2}(u_1 + u_n)$

   $\Rightarrow S_{100} = \dfrac{100}{2}(1 + 100) = 5050$

Going for the top 2

1. (a) Here $PV = 500$, $FV = 700$, $n = 2$ and $k = 1$.

   $700 = 500 \times \left(1 + \dfrac{r}{100}\right)^2$

   $\Rightarrow 1 + \dfrac{r}{100} = \sqrt{\dfrac{7}{5}}$

   $\Rightarrow r = 100\left(\sqrt{\dfrac{7}{5}} - 1\right) = 18.3$ (3 SF)

   (Alternatively, use a financial app on the GDC to solve for r.)

   So the annual interest rate is 18.3%.

   (b) Taking $PV = 500$, $r = 18.3$, $n = 5$ and $k = 1$:

   $FV = 500 \times \left(1 + \dfrac{18.3}{100}\right)^5 = 1158.49$ (2 DP)

   Or, using the more accurate value of $r = 18.32159566$:

   $FV = 500 \times \left(1 + \dfrac{18.32159566}{100}\right)^5 = 1159.55$ (2 DP)

   So Mr Liu will owe around \$1159 after 5 years.

2. Brian's pocket money follows a geometric sequence with $u_1 = 10$ and $r = 1.2$, so in the nth year after his 8th birthday, he is getting $u_n = 10 \times 1.2^{n-1}$ pounds per week.

   Sandra's pocket money follows an arithmetic sequence with $v_1 = 15$ and $d = 1$, so in the nth year after her 8th birthday, she is getting $v_n = 15 + 1(n-1)$ pounds per week.

   (a) We want to find when $u_n > v_n$. From the table on the GDC, the smallest n for this occurs is $n = 5$.

   In the 5th year after their 8th birthdays, they will be 12 years old.

   (b) In the first year they are 8 years old, so the last year before they turn 18 will be the 10th year, i.e. $n = 10$.

   - For Brian: In the first year he gets $52 \times 10 = 520$ in total.
     An annual increase of 20% means that $r = 1.2$.
     So after 10 years he gets a total of
     $S_{10} = \dfrac{520(1.2^{10} - 1)}{1.2 - 1} = \pounds 13\,498.51$

   - For Sandra: In the first year she gets $52 \times 15 = 780$ in total.
     Each year the total she receives increases by $52 \times 1 = 52$, so $d = 52$.
     After 10 years she gets a total of
     $S_{10} = \dfrac{10}{2}(2 \times 780 + 9 \times 52) = \pounds 10\,140$

3 DESCRIPTIVE STATISTICS

Mixed practice 3

1. (a) There are two 2s, two 5s and two 6s, so for 5 to be the mode there must be one more of them. Hence $x = 5$.

   (b) Writing the numbers in order: 1, 2, 2, 3, 4, 5, 5, 5, 6, 6. There are ten numbers, so the median is the mean of the 5th and 6th numbers: $\frac{4+5}{2} = 4.5$.

2. (a) School 1: IQR = 41 − 26 = 15

   School 2: IQR = 48 − 34 = 14

   (b)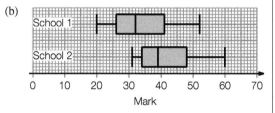

   (c) The results have a similar spread. The results for School 2 are better on average.

3. (a) Using the formula $\bar{x} = \dfrac{\sum\limits_{i=1}^{k} f_i x_i}{n}$ where $n = \sum\limits_{i=1}^{k} f_i$,

   the mean is $\dfrac{3 \times 4 + 4 \times 12 + 5x + 6 \times 17 + 7 \times 9}{4 + 12 + x + 17 + 9}$. So

   $$\frac{12 + 48 + 5x + 102 + 63}{42 + x} = 5.23$$
   $$\Leftrightarrow 225 + 5x = 5.23(42 + x)$$
   $$\Leftrightarrow 225 - 219.66 = 0.23x$$
   $$\Leftrightarrow x = \frac{5.34}{0.23}$$
   $$\therefore x = 23 \quad (\text{as } x \text{ must be an integer})$$

   (b) There are 65 students, so the median is the 33rd number, which is 5.

4. (a) Calculate the cumulative frequency up to each upper class boundary:

Speed (km/h)	Number of cars	Cumulative frequency
< **140**	0	0
140–**160**	14	14
160–**175**	35	49
175–**185**	41	90
185–**190**	23	113
190–**200**	17	130

Then plot the cumulative frequency graph:

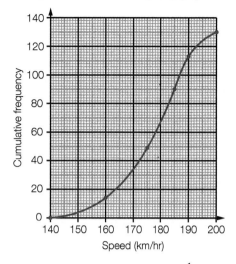

   (b) The total frequency is 130, and $\frac{1}{4} \times 130 = 32.5$, $\frac{1}{2} \times 130 = 65$ and $\frac{3}{4} \times 130 = 97.5$.

   From the cumulative frequency curve, by drawing lines from 32.5, 65 and 97.5 on the vertical axis, one finds:

   $Q_1 \approx 169$, Median ≈ 179, $Q_3 \approx 186$

   We also know that Min = 140 and Max = 200 for the data.

   Plot these 5 figures on a box and whisker diagram:

   (c) IQR = $Q_3 - Q_1$ = 186 − 169 = 17

5. (a) Calculate the frequency table:

Age x (years)	Frequency
$16 \le x \le 26$	12
$26 < x \le 36$	46 − 12 = 34
$36 < x \le 46$	82 − 46 = 36
$46 < x \le 56$	90 − 82 = 8

Then use this information to draw the histogram:

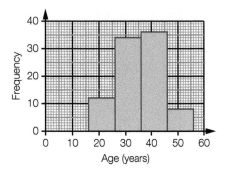

(b) The frequencies are: **12**, 46 − 12 = **34**, 82 − 46 = **36**, 90 − 82 = **8**.

Using the mid-interval values of the age brackets:

Mid-interval values	Frequency
21	12
31	34
41	36
51	8

From GDC, mean = 35.4 years and standard deviation = 8.31 years

6. (a) Frequencies: 6, 8, 14, 10, 3, 5

(b) Using the mid-interval values of each class:

Distance (cm)	450.5	470.5	490.5	510.5	530.5	550.5
Frequency	6	8	14	10	3	5

From GDC, mean = 495 cm and standard deviation = 28.9 cm

(c) Calculate the cumulative frequency up to each upper class boundary:

Distance (cm)	Frequency	Cumulative frequency
≤ **440**	0	0
441–**460**	6	6
461–**480**	8	14
481–**500**	14	28
501–**520**	10	38
521–**540**	3	41
541–**560**	5	46

Then plot the cumulative frequency graph:

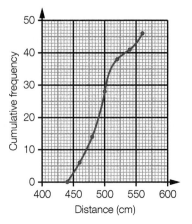

(d) (i) From the graph, a distance of 480 cm corresponds to a cumulative frequency of 14. So there are 46 − 14 = 32 athletes who jumped more than 480 cm; this corresponds to a percentage of $\frac{32}{46} \times 100\% = 69.6\%$.

(ii) The probability of each athlete jumping further than 480 cm is $\frac{32}{46}$, so the probability that the two athletes both jumped more than 480 cm is $\frac{32}{46} \times \frac{32}{46} \approx 0.484$.

(e) 20% of 46 is 9.2, so the lower 80% of the athletes correspond to a cumulative frequency of 46 − 9.2 = 36.8. From the graph in (c), a cumulative frequency of 36.8 corresponds to a distance of 515 cm. Therefore, the minimum distance required for qualification is 5.15 m.

Going for the top 3

1. Since there are 36 pieces of data,
$$9 + 13 + x + y = 36$$
$$\Rightarrow x + y = 14 \quad \cdots (1)$$

Since the mean is $\frac{47}{9}$,

$$\frac{4 \times 9 + 5 \times 13 + 6x + 7y}{9 + 13 + x + y} = \frac{47}{9}$$
$$\Rightarrow 9(101 + 6x + 7y) = 47(22 + x + y)$$
$$\Rightarrow 909 + 54x + 63y = 1034 + 47x + 47y$$
$$\Rightarrow 7x + 16y = 125 \quad \cdots (2)$$

Solving (1) and (2) simultaneously gives $x = 11$, $y = 3$.

2. Among the known numbers there are two 3s and two 7s. Since the mode is 3, there must be another 3.

Therefore at least one of x, y and z must be 3. Let us take $x = 3$.

There are 11 numbers, so the median is the 6th number. As there are no 6s among the numbers known so far, one of the remaining unknowns must be 6. Let us take $y = 6$.

The mean is 6, i.e.

$$\frac{3+2+3+7+10+5+7+12+3+6+z}{11} = 6$$

$$\Rightarrow 58 + z = 66$$

$$\Rightarrow z = 8$$

Therefore x, y and z are 3, 6 and 8.

3. (a) (i) $15 + 20 + 10 = 45$ students

        (ii) 37 is two-fifths of the way from 35 to 40, so we can estimate that three-fifths of this group take more than 37 minutes; this corresponds to $\frac{3}{5} \times 10 = 6$ students.

    (b) $\frac{6}{45} \approx 0.133$

4 SET THEORY AND VENN DIAGRAMS

Mixed practice 4

1. (a) $S = \{1, 4, 9, 16\}$ and $E = \{2, 4, 6, 8, 10, 12, 14, 16, 18\}$

        So $S \cap E = \{4, 16\}$

    (b) $S \cup E' = \{1, 3, 4, 5, 7, 9, 11, 13, 15, 16, 17, 19\}$, so $n(S \cup E') = 12$.

2. Venn diagrams only: $32 - 24 = 8$ papers

    Currency conversion only: $30 - 24 = 6$ papers

    Therefore, the number of papers that contain neither topic is $40 - (8 + 24 + 6) = 2$

3.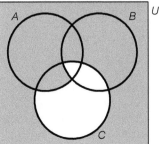

4. The number of students who study French or Spanish is the total number of students less the number who study neither language: $n(F \cup S) = 30 - 8 = 22$

    So $n(F \cap S) = n(F) + n(S) - n(F \cup S) = 22 + 17 - 22 = 17$

    Alternatively, let x be the number of students who study both French and Spanish. Then the number who study French only is $22 - x$, and the number who study Spanish only is $17 - x$.

    Thus $(22 - x) + (17 - x) + x + 8 = 30$ and solving this equation gives $x = 17$.

5. $n(A \cap B) = 0$ means that in the Venn diagram, A and B should be represented by circles that do not overlap.

    The set $A' \cap B'$ is everything in U that does not belong to either A or B.

    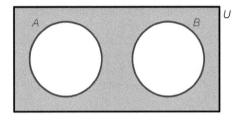

6. Starting with the information that no students did all three activities (0 in the central overlap of all three sets), we can draw the following Venn diagram:

    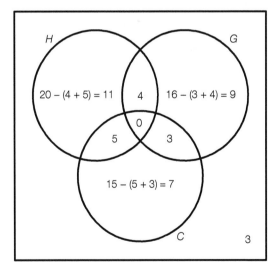

    (a) The total number of students is $11 + 4 + 9 + 5 + 3 + 7 + 3 = 42$

    (b) 11 students only did homework, so the percentage is $\frac{11}{42} \times 100\% = 26.2\%$

1. (a) Let $A = \{a, b, c\}$; then its non-empty proper subsets are:

$\{a\}, \{b\}, \{c\}, \{a, b\}, \{b, c\}, \{c, a\}$

So A has 6 proper subsets.

(b) Let $A = \{a, b, c, d\}$; then its non-empty proper subsets are:

$\{a\}, \{b\}, \{c\}, \{d\},$

$\{a, b\}, \{a, c\}, \{a, d\}, \{b, c\}, \{b, d\}, \{c, d\},$

$\{a, b, c\}, \{a, b, d\}, \{a, c, d\}, \{b, c, d\}$

So A has 14 proper subsets.

(c) Consider a subset of a set of size n. For each element of the original set, there are two options: either it is in this subset, or it is not. So there are 2 choices for each of n elements, making 2^n possibilities altogether; hence there are 2^n possible subsets. However, two of those are the empty set and the whole set, so the number of non-empty proper subsets is $2^n - 2$.

2. Let n be the number of students who read all three authors. We can draw the Venn diagram (starting from the middle and working outwards):

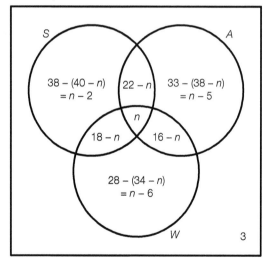

Since the total number of students is 50,

$(n - 2) + (22 - n) + (n - 5) + (18 - n) + n + (16 - n)$

$+ (n - 6) + 3 = 50$

$\Leftrightarrow n + 46 = 50$

$\Leftrightarrow n = 4$

5 LOGIC

Mixed practice 5

1. (a) (i) The number ends in 2 or it is even.

(ii) If the number ends in 2, then it is even.

(iii) If the number does not end in 2, then it is not even.

(b) (i) $q \Rightarrow p$　　(ii) $\neg q \Rightarrow \neg p$

2. (a) (i)

p	q	$\neg p$	$p \wedge q$	$(p \wedge q) \wedge \neg p$
T	T	F	T	F
T	F	F	F	F
F	T	T	F	F
F	F	T	F	F

(ii)

p	q	$\neg p$	$\neg p \vee q$
T	T	F	T
T	F	F	F
F	T	T	T
F	F	T	T

(iii)

p	q	$\neg p$	$p \vee \neg p$	$(p \vee \neg p) \vee q$
T	T	F	T	T
T	F	F	T	T
F	T	T	T	T
F	F	T	T	T

(iv)

p	q	$p \Rightarrow q$
T	T	T
T	F	F
F	T	T
F	F	T

(b) (i) $(p \wedge q) \wedge \neg p$　　(ii) $(p \vee \neg p) \vee q$

(iii) $\neg p \vee q$ and $p \Rightarrow q$

3. (a) (i) 'Neither John nor Iqbal studies mathematics' means that John is **not** studying mathematics **and** Iqbal is **not** studying mathematics, i.e. $\neg p \wedge \neg q$.

(ii) If John and Iqbal are **both** studying mathematics, this would be $p \wedge q$. So if it is **not** the case that they are both studying mathematics, we express this as $\neg(p \wedge q)$.

(iii) $p \Leftrightarrow q$

(b) Either John or Iqbal is studying mathematics, but not both.

4. (a) Start with three columns for the initial propositions p, q and r, with 8 rows showing the different combinations of T and F for the three propositions. Then add columns for $p \Rightarrow q$ and $q \Rightarrow r$, and finally a column for $(p \Rightarrow q) \wedge (q \Rightarrow r)$.

p	q	r	$p \Rightarrow q$	$q \Rightarrow r$	$(p \Rightarrow q) \wedge (q \Rightarrow r)$
T	T	T	T	T	T
T	T	F	T	F	F
T	F	T	F	T	F
T	F	F	F	T	F
F	T	T	T	T	T
F	T	F	T	F	F
F	F	T	T	T	T
F	F	F	T	T	T

(b) $p \Rightarrow r$ is true when both p and r are true, so it would have a T in the third row, whereas the above table has an F in the third row of the final column. Hence $p \Rightarrow r$ is not logically equivalent to $(p \Rightarrow q) \wedge (q \Rightarrow r)$.

5. (a)

p	q	$\neg p$	$\neg q$	$p \vee q$	$\neg p \wedge \neg q$	$(p \vee q) \wedge (\neg p \wedge \neg q)$
T	T	F	F	T	F	F
T	F	F	T	T	F	F
F	T	T	F	T	F	F
F	F	T	T	F	T	F

(b) The final column consists entirely of Fs, so the statement is a contradiction.

6. (a)

p	q	$p \Rightarrow q$
T	T	T
T	F	F
F	T	T
F	F	T

(b)

p	q	$\neg q$	$p \Rightarrow \neg q$	$((p \Rightarrow q) \wedge (p \Rightarrow \neg q))$	$\neg p$	$((p \Rightarrow q) \wedge (p \Rightarrow \neg q)) \Rightarrow \neg p$
T	T	F	F	F	F	T
T	F	T	T	F	F	T
F	T	F	T	T	T	T
F	F	T	T	T	T	T

The final column is all T, so the implication is a tautology, and hence the argument is valid.

7. (a) (i) $\neg q \Rightarrow \neg p$

(ii) The contrapositive of the statement $\neg q \Rightarrow \neg p$ is $p \Rightarrow q$, which in words is: 'If the object is a square then it is a rectangle.'

(b)

p	q	$p \wedge q$	$p \wedge q \Rightarrow p$
T	T	T	T
T	F	F	T
F	T	F	T
F	F	F	T

The final column is all T, so the implication is a tautology, and hence the argument is valid.

(c) $p \Rightarrow q$ is valid: if an object is a square then it is also a rectangle (since a square is a special type of rectangle). $q \Rightarrow p$ is not valid; a rectangle need not be a square.

Going for the top 5

1. Inverse: $\neg p \Rightarrow q$; Converse: $\neg q \Rightarrow p$; Contrapositive: $q \Rightarrow \neg p$

2. (a)

p	q	$\neg p$	$\neg p \vee q$	$p \Rightarrow q$
T	T	F	T	T
T	F	F	F	F
F	T	T	T	T
F	F	T	T	T

Since the columns for $\neg p \vee q$ and $p \Rightarrow q$ are identical, the two statements are logically equivalent.

(b) $p \Leftrightarrow q$ is the same as '$p \Rightarrow q$ and $q \Rightarrow p$'.

From (a), $p \Rightarrow q$ is logically equivalent to $\neg p \vee q$; analogously, $q \Rightarrow p$ is logically equivalent to $\neg q \vee p$.

Hence, $p \Leftrightarrow q$ is logically equivalent to $(\neg p \vee q) \wedge (\neg q \vee p)$.

3. (a)

p	q	$p \Rightarrow q$	$\neg q$	$\neg p$	$\neg q \Rightarrow \neg p$	$(p \Rightarrow q) \Rightarrow$ $(\neg q \Rightarrow \neg p)$
T	T	T	F	F	T	T
T	F	F	T	F	F	T
F	T	T	F	T	T	T
F	F	T	T	T	T	T

The last column contains only Ts, so the argument is valid.

(b) It says that if an implication is true then its contrapositive is also true.

4. We need to show that $p \vee (q \wedge r)$ is logically equivalent to $(p \vee q) \wedge (p \vee r)$.

p	q	r	$q \wedge r$	$p \vee (q \wedge r)$	$p \vee q$	$p \vee r$	$(p \vee q) \wedge$ $(p \vee r)$
T	T	T	T	T	T	T	T
T	T	F	F	T	T	T	T
T	F	T	F	T	T	T	T
T	F	F	F	T	T	T	T
F	T	T	T	T	T	T	T
F	T	F	F	F	T	F	F
F	F	T	F	F	F	T	F
F	F	F	F	F	F	F	F

The two shaded columns are identical, so the two statements are logically equivalent.

6 PROBABILITY

Mixed practice 6

1. (a) There are $10 + 14 = 24$ marbles in total. The probability of choosing a red one is $\frac{10}{24} = \frac{5}{12}$.

(b) The following tree diagram shows the possible outcomes for the two choices:

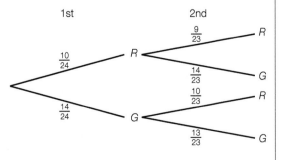

(i) $\frac{10}{24} \times \frac{9}{23} = 0.163$

(ii) P(different colours)

$= $ P(red, green OR green, red)

$= $ P(red, green) + P(green, red)

$= \left(\frac{10}{24} \times \frac{14}{23} \right) + \left(\frac{14}{24} \times \frac{10}{23} \right) = 0.507$

2. (a) $8 + 6 + 0 + 8 + 10 + 6 + 1 + 3 + 5 = 47$

(b) (i) $\frac{0 + 6 + 5}{47} = \frac{11}{47}$ (ii) $\frac{1 + 3 + 5}{47} = \frac{9}{47}$

(iii) $\frac{5}{1 + 3 + 5} = \frac{5}{9}$

(iv) Scoring 'at least one goal' includes scoring one goal and scoring more than one goal, so P(draw | at least one goal) $=$ $\frac{10 + 3}{8 + 10 + 6 + 1 + 3 + 5} = \frac{13}{33}$

3. (a) $0.4 \times 0.4 = 0.16$

(b) Consider the following tree diagram:

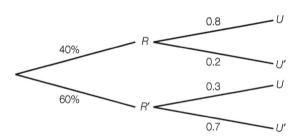

P(takes umbrella) = P(rains and takes umbrella OR doesn't rain and takes umbrella)

$= $ P(rains and takes umbrella)
$+ $ P(doesn't rain and takes umbrella)

$= 0.4 \times 0.8 + 0.6 \times 0.3 = 0.5$

4. (a) $360° - (4 \times 40° + 70° + 50° + 60°) = 20°$

(b) $\frac{20}{360} = \frac{1}{18}$

(c) $\frac{20}{70 + 50 + 60 + 20} = \frac{20}{200} = 0.1$

5. (a)

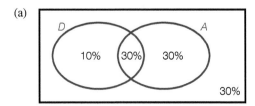

(b) $10\% = 0.1$

(c) $P(D\,|\,A) = \dfrac{0.3}{0.6} = 0.5$

6. (a) $10 + 13 + 13 + 12 + 11 + 15 = 74$

(b) (i) $\dfrac{12 + 11 + 15}{74} = 0.514$

(ii) $\dfrac{13}{74} = 0.176$

(iii) $\dfrac{12 + 11 + 15 + 13}{74} = 0.689$

(c) $\dfrac{10}{10 + 13 + 13} = 0.278$

(d) $P(\text{first student from group C}) = \dfrac{28}{74}$

Because the same student cannot be selected twice,
$P(\text{both students from group C}) = \dfrac{28}{74} \times \dfrac{27}{73} = 0.140$

Going for the top 6

1. $P(\text{neither pink nor dress}) = 1 - P(\text{pink} \cup \text{dress})$
$= 1 - (P(\text{pink}) + P(\text{dress})$
$- P(\text{pink} \cap \text{dress}))$

Since the two properties are independent,
$P(\text{pink} \cap \text{dress}) = P(\text{pink}) \times P(\text{dress})$
$= 0.3 \times 0.6 = 0.18$

$\therefore\ P(\text{neither pink nor dress}) = 1 - (0.3 + 0.6 - 0.18) = 0.28$

2. (a) There are $12 + 20 + 18 = 50$ balls in total.

$P(\text{all 3 same colour})$
$= P(3\ \text{red}\ \text{OR}\ 3\ \text{green}\ \text{OR}\ 3\ \text{blue})$
$= P(3\ \text{red}) + P(3\ \text{green}) + P(3\ \text{blue})$
$= \dfrac{12}{50} \times \dfrac{11}{49} \times \dfrac{10}{48} + \dfrac{20}{50} \times \dfrac{19}{49} \times \dfrac{18}{48}$
$+ \dfrac{18}{50} \times \dfrac{17}{49} \times \dfrac{16}{48} = 0.111$

(b) There are 6 different orders in which the 3 colours can be picked (RGB, RBG, GRB, GBR, BRG, BGR), and each of these has a probability of
$\dfrac{12 \times 20 \times 18}{50 \times 49 \times 48} = 0.0367.$

Hence, $P(\text{all 3 different colours}) = 6 \times 0.0367 = 0.220.$

(c) Using the conditional probability formula:

$P(\text{3rd blue}\,|\,\text{first 2 blue}) = \dfrac{P(\text{all 3 blue})}{P(\text{first 2 blue})}$

$= \dfrac{\dfrac{18}{50} \times \dfrac{17}{49} \times \dfrac{16}{48}}{\dfrac{18}{50} \times \dfrac{17}{49}}$

$= \dfrac{16}{48} = \dfrac{1}{3} = 0.333$

(Note that there is a more direct way to get to the answer: given that the first two balls are blue, there are then 16 blue balls left out of the total of 48. Hence, the probability that the third ball is also blue is $\dfrac{16}{48}$.)

(d) Listing all the ways that the third ball can be red, and adding their probabilities:

$P(\text{RRR or RGR or RBR or GRR or GGR}$
$\text{or GBR or BRR or BGR or BBR})$
$= \dfrac{12 \times 11 \times 10}{50 \times 49 \times 48} + \dfrac{12 \times 20 \times 11}{50 \times 49 \times 48} + \dfrac{12 \times 18 \times 11}{50 \times 49 \times 48}$
$+ \dfrac{20 \times 12 \times 11}{50 \times 49 \times 48} + \dfrac{20 \times 19 \times 12}{50 \times 49 \times 48} + \dfrac{20 \times 18 \times 12}{50 \times 49 \times 48}$
$+ \dfrac{18 \times 12 \times 11}{50 \times 49 \times 48} + \dfrac{18 \times 20 \times 12}{50 \times 49 \times 48} + \dfrac{18 \times 17 \times 12}{50 \times 49 \times 48}$
$= \dfrac{6}{25} = 0.24$

(More directly, we can argue that with no restrictions on the first two balls,
$P(\text{3rd is Red}) = P(\text{1st is Red}) = \dfrac{12}{50} = 0.24.$)

7 STATISTICAL APPLICATIONS

Mixed practice 7

1. (a) A (strong positive correlation)

(b) C (negative correlation)

(c) B (no linear correlation)

2. (a) From GDC, $r = 0.840$

(b) From GDC, $l = 3.61m + 38.0$

(c) For $m = 3.2$, predict $l = 3.61 \times 3.2 + 38.0 = 49.6\,\text{cm}$

(d) No; 5.6 is outside the range of the mass data (extrapolation is unreliable).

3. (a) From GDC: (i) $P(3.2 \le m \le 4.8) = 0.446;$

(ii) $P(m > 5.0) = 0.369$

(b) From (a)(i), $P(m < 5.0) = 1 - 0.369 = 0.631$

For two dogs, A and B:

P(one of A or B has $m > 5$)

= P(A has $m > 5$ and B has $m < 5$
OR   A has $m < 5$ and B has $m > 5$)

= P(A has $m > 5$ and B has $m < 5$)
  + P(A has $m < 5$ and B has $m > 5$)

= $0.369 \times 0.631 + 0.631 \times 0.369 = 0.466$

4. (a) Using the mid-interval values:

Time	2.5	7.5	12.5	17.5	22.5
Frequency	3	9	13	10	5

From GDC: mean = 13.1 minutes, standard deviation = 5.61 minutes

(b) For mean: $\dfrac{16 - 13.1}{16} \times 100 = 18.1\%$

For standard deviation: $\dfrac{6 - 5.61}{6} \times 100 = 6.5\%$

(c) $X \sim N(16, 6^2)$

From GDC, $P(X > 30) = 0.00982$, so 0.982% of students take more than half an hour.

5. (a) There are 228 children in the group, so:

(i) $\dfrac{21}{228} = 0.0921$ (ii) $\dfrac{54 + 32 + 71}{228} = 0.689$

(b) H_0: Hair colour and eye colour are independent.

H_1: Hair colour and eye colour are dependent.

(c) Expected frequencies can be calculated as follows (or by using your GDC):

	Fair	Dark
Blue	$\dfrac{86 \times 71}{228} = 26.8$	$\dfrac{86 \times 157}{228} = 59.2$
Green	$\dfrac{50 \times 71}{228} = 15.6$	$\dfrac{50 \times 157}{228} = 34.4$
Brown	$\dfrac{92 \times 71}{228} = 26.6$	$\dfrac{92 \times 157}{228} = 63.4$

Degrees of freedom = $(2 - 1) \times (3 - 1) = 2$

From GDC: $\chi^2_{calc} = 4.99, p = 0.0823$

$p > 0.05$, so there is not sufficient evidence to reject H_0; that is, there is insufficient evidence that hair colour and eye colour are dependent.

6. (a) (Strong) positive correlation

(b) From the scatter diagram: $A = 7.8, B = 6.1$

(c) From GDC: $\bar{l} = 7.58$ cm, $\bar{w} = 5.68$ cm

(d) (The line of best fit should pass through the mean point, with gradient about 1.)

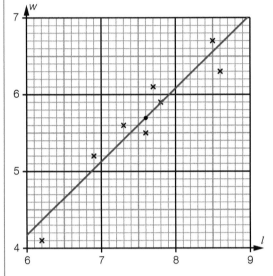

Going for the top 7

1. (a)

$X \sim N(5, \sigma^2)$

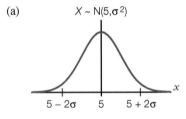

(b) Note that 3 and 7 are symmetrical about the mean 5.

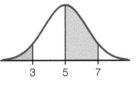

From the diagram, and using the symmetry of the normal curve:

$P(5 < X < 7) = P(3 < X < 5)$
$= 0.5 - P(X < 3)$
$= 0.5 - 0.06 = 0.44$

2. **(a)** When $M = 250$:

$$123 + 2.6a = 250$$
$$\Rightarrow 2.6a = 127$$
$$\Rightarrow a = 48.85$$

So they need to spend 48.85 USD.

(b) It is the number of members the club is expected to have if they spend no money on advertising.

3. **(a)** Chi-squared test.

H_0: The favourite sport is independent of nationality.

H_1: The favourite sport is dependent on nationality.

(b) Totals from the table are:

	Basketball	Soccer	Total
Brazilian	26	54	**80**
Mexican	31	47	**78**
Indian	51	33	**84**
Total	**108**	**134**	**242**

(i) $P(\text{Brazilian}) = \dfrac{80}{242} = 0.331$

(ii) $P(\text{prefers basketball}) = \dfrac{108}{242} = 0.446$

(c) The expected number of students who are Brazilian and prefer basketball is $0.331 \times 0.446 \times 242 = 35.7$.

(d) Expected frequencies are:

	Basketball	Soccer
Brazilian	35.7	44.3
Mexican	34.8	43.2
Indian	37.5	46.5

Degrees of freedom $= (3 - 1) \times (2 - 1) = 2$

From GDC: $\chi^2_{calc} = 14.3$, $p = 7.81 \times 10^{-4}$

$p < 0.1$, so at the 10% significance level there is sufficient evidence to reject H_0; that is, there is evidence that the favourite sport depends on nationality.

4. **(a)** From the histogram, using mid-interval values:

Score	45	55	65	75	85	95
Frequency	10	20	30	30	20	10

From GDC: mean = 70, standard deviation = 13.8

(b) Within one standard deviation of the mean is between $70 - 13.8 = 56.2$ and $70 + 13.8 = 83.8$.

From the histogram, the number of students scoring between 56 and 84 is estimated to be:

$$\left(\frac{4}{10} \times 20\right) + 30 + 30 + \left(\frac{4}{10} \times 20\right) = 76$$

(c) A normal distribution has about 68% of data within one standard deviation of the mean.

$\dfrac{76}{120} \times 100\% = 63.3\%$, which is significantly less than 68%.

Therefore, the normal distribution is not a suitable model for these test scores.

8 GEOMETRY AND TRIGONOMETRY

Mixed practice 8

1. **(a)** Using the cosine rule in triangle ABC:

$$AB^2 = AC^2 + BC^2 - 2 \times AC \times BC \cos 120°$$
$$= 12^2 + 12^2 - 2(12)(12)\cos 120°$$
$$= 432$$

$\therefore AB = 20.8$ cm

(b) Shaded area = area of sector ABC − area of triangle ABC

$$= \frac{120}{360} \times \pi \times 12^2 - \frac{1}{2} \times 12 \times 12 \sin 120°$$
$$= 88.4 \text{ cm}^2$$

(c) Area of circle $= \pi \times 12^2 = 144\pi$

Percentage error in estimate

$$= \left| \frac{\frac{1}{6} \times \text{area of circle} - \text{area of triangle}}{\text{area of triangle}} \right| \times 100\%$$

$$= \left| \frac{\frac{1}{6} \times 144\pi - \frac{1}{2} \times 12 \times 12 \sin 120°}{\frac{1}{2} \times 12 \times 12 \sin 120°} \right| \times 100\%$$

$$= 20.9\%$$

2. (a) Surface area $= \pi r^2 + \pi rl$

$\therefore 707 = \pi \times 9^2 + \pi \times 9l$

$\Rightarrow l = \dfrac{707 - 81\pi}{9\pi} = 16.0$ cm

(b) By Pythagoras' theorem,

$h^2 + 9^2 = l^2$, so

$h = \sqrt{l^2 - r^2}$

$\quad = \sqrt{(16.005...)^2 - 9^2}$

$\quad = 13.2$ cm

$V = \dfrac{1}{3}\pi r^2 h$

$\quad = \dfrac{1}{3}\pi \times 9^2 \times 13.2$

$\quad = 1120$ cm^3 (3 SF)

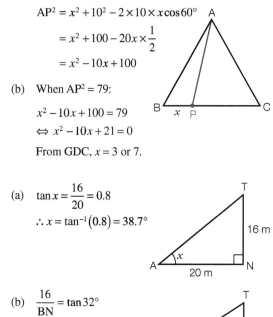

3. (a) $h^2 = 7^2 - 4^2 = 33$

$\therefore h = 5.74$ cm

Area $= \dfrac{1}{2}\left(8 \times \sqrt{33}\right)$

$\quad = 22.978...$

$\quad = 23.0$ cm^2

(b) $H^2 = h^2 - 4^2 = 33 - 16 = 17$

$\therefore H = 4.1231...$

$\quad = 4.12$ cm (3 SF)

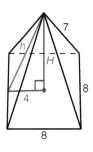

(c) Total volume = volume of cuboid + volume of pyramid

$= 8^2 \times 26 + \dfrac{1}{3}(8^2 \times H)$

$= 1751.95...$

$= 1750$ cm^3 (3 SF)

(d) Surface area of lid $= 4 \times 22.978... = 91.9$ cm^2

Surface area of body $= 8^2 + 4 \times (26 \times 8)$

$= 896$ cm^2

$\therefore$ percentage of total material used for lid

$= \dfrac{91.9}{91.9 + 896} \times 100\% = 9.30\%$

4. (a) Using the cosine rule in triangle ABP:

$AP^2 = x^2 + 10^2 - 2 \times 10 \times x \cos 60°$

$\quad = x^2 + 100 - 20x \times \dfrac{1}{2}$

$\quad = x^2 - 10x + 100$

(b) When $AP^2 = 79$:

$x^2 - 10x + 100 = 79$

$\Leftrightarrow x^2 - 10x + 21 = 0$

From GDC, $x = 3$ or 7.

5. (a) $\tan x = \dfrac{16}{20} = 0.8$

$\therefore x = \tan^{-1}(0.8) = 38.7°$

(b) $\dfrac{16}{BN} = \tan 32°$

$\Rightarrow BN = \dfrac{16}{\tan 32°}$

$\quad = 25.6$ m

(c) Using the cosine rule in triangle ABN:

$\cos A\widehat{N}B = \dfrac{20^2 + 25.6^2 - 12^2}{2(20)(25.6)}$

$\quad = 0.890$

$\therefore A\widehat{N}B = \cos^{-1}(0.890)$

$\quad = 27.1°$

6. (a) (i) $3x + 2y = 6$

$\Rightarrow y = -\dfrac{3}{2}x + 3$

So gradient of l_1 is $m_1 = -\dfrac{3}{2}$.

(ii) When l_1 crosses the y-axis, $x = 0$. Substituting 0 for x in the equation for l_1 gives $y = 3$.

So M has coordinates $(0, 3)$.

(b) Since l_2 is perpendicular to l_1, its gradient is

$$m_2 = \frac{-1}{-\frac{3}{2}} = \frac{2}{3}$$

So the equation of l_2 is

$$y - y_1 = m(x - x_1)$$

$$y - (-8) = \frac{2}{3}(x - 3)$$

$$\Rightarrow 3y + 24 = 2x - 6$$

$$\Rightarrow 2x - 3y - 30 = 0$$

(c) For the point of intersection of l_1 and l_2, solve simultaneously the equations

$$3x + 2y - 6 = 0$$

$$2x - 3y - 30 = 0$$

From GDC, N has coordinates $(6, -6)$.

(d) $NM = \sqrt{(6-0)^2 + (-6-3)^2} = \sqrt{117} = 10.8$

$NP = \sqrt{(6-3)^2 + (-6-(-8))^2} = \sqrt{13} = 3.61$

(e)

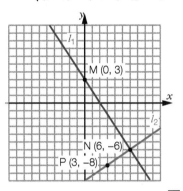

Since $P\widehat{N}M = 90°$, $\tan(P\widehat{M}N) = \dfrac{\sqrt{13}}{\sqrt{117}}$

$\therefore P\widehat{M}N = \tan^{-1}\left(\dfrac{\sqrt{13}}{\sqrt{117}}\right) = 18.4°$

(f) Area $= \dfrac{1}{2} \times \sqrt{13} \times \sqrt{117} = 19.5$

Going for the top 8

1. (a) Let l denote the length of a slanted edge.

$$\sin 72° = \frac{26}{l}$$

$$\Rightarrow l = \frac{26}{\sin 72°}$$

$$= 27.3 \text{ cm}$$

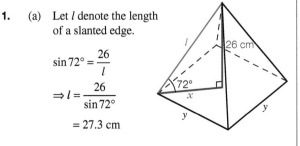

(b) $\tan 72° = \dfrac{26}{x} \Rightarrow x = \dfrac{26}{\tan 72°} = 8.45$ cm

So length of diagonal $= 2x = 16.9$ cm

(c) To find the volume, we first need to find the area of the square base.

By Pythagoras' theorem,

$$16.9^2 = y^2 + y^2$$

$$\Rightarrow y^2 = 142.7$$

Therefore,

$$\text{Volume} = \frac{1}{3} y^2 h$$

$$= \frac{1}{3} \times 142.7 \times 26$$

$$= 1240 \text{ cm}^3 \ (3 \text{ SF})$$

2. (a) $V = \pi r^2 h$

$\therefore 200 = \pi r^2 h$

$\Rightarrow h = \dfrac{200}{\pi r^2}$

(b) The outer surface area consists of the area of the base and the area of the curved side:

$S = \pi r^2 + 2\pi r h$

$= \pi r^2 + 2\pi r\left(\dfrac{200}{\pi r^2}\right)$ (using part (a))

$= \pi r^2 + \dfrac{400}{r}$

(c) Plotting S against r on the GDC, the minimum point on the graph is at $r = 3.99$ cm.

9 FUNCTIONS, EQUATIONS AND MATHEMATICAL MODELS

Mixed practice 9

1. A: Quadratic function with negative coefficient of x^2; therefore $y = c - x^2$

B: Straight line (with negative gradient); therefore $y = a - x$

C: Exponential growth function (with positive gradient); therefore $y = 3 + n^x$

D: Exponential decay function (with negative gradient); therefore $y = k + 5^{-x}$

E: Rational function (with vertical asymptote at $x = 0$); therefore $y = bx^{-1}$

F: Quadratic function with positive coefficient of x^2; therefore $y = x^2 + m$

2. Area $= (x-3)(x+5)$, so:

$(x-3)(x+5) = 68$

$\Leftrightarrow x^2 + 2x - 83 = 0$

$\Leftrightarrow x = 8.17$ or -10.2 (from GDC)

As $x > 0$, $x = 8.17$.

3.

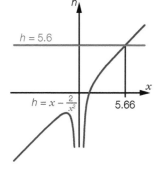

(a) From GDC: $h(3.2) = 3.00$

(b) From GDC, the solution of $h(x) = 5.6$ is $x = 5.66$

4. (a) $f(1) = 5 \Rightarrow 3a + \dfrac{b}{1} = 5$

$\Rightarrow 3a + b = 5$ $\cdots$ (1)

$f(2) = 5 \Rightarrow 9a + \dfrac{b}{2} = 5$

$\Rightarrow 18a + b = 10$ $\cdots$ (2)

Solving (1) and (2) simultaneously (e.g. using the GDC) gives $a = \dfrac{1}{3}$, $b = 4$.

(b) From GDC, the solutions of $f(x) = 7$ are $x = 0.632$ and $x = 2.54$.

(c) From GDC, the minimum point is at $(1.47, 4.40)$.

5. (a) When $m = 0$, $T = 5$, so $5 = c - k \times 1.2^0$

$\Rightarrow c - k = 5$ $\cdots$ (1)

When $m = 5$, $T = 15$, so $15 = c - k \times 1.2^{-5}$

$\Rightarrow c - 1.2^{-5}k = 15$ $\cdots$ (2)

Solving (1) and (2) simultaneously with a GDC gives $c = 21.7$, $k = 16.7$.

(b) Substituting in the values for c and k, we have the equation $T = 21.7 - 16.7 \times 1.2^{-m}$.

$T = 20 \Rightarrow 21.7 - 16.7 \times 1.2^{-m} = 20$.

Solving this equation with the GDC gives $m = 12.5$, i.e. it takes 12.5 minutes.

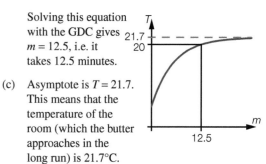

(c) Asymptote is $T = 21.7$. This means that the temperature of the room (which the butter approaches in the long run) is $21.7°C$.

Going for the top 9

1. A quadratic function has equation $y = a(x-p)(x-q)$, where p and q are the roots (x-intercepts of the graph).

From the graph, there are roots -2 and 8, so $y = a(x+2)(x-8)$

When $x = 3$, $y = 32$, so $a(3+2)(3-8) = 32$

$\Rightarrow -25a = 32$

$\Rightarrow a = -\dfrac{32}{25} = -1.28$

Therefore, the equation is $y = -1.28(x+2)(x-8) = -1.28x^2 + 7.68x + 20.48$

2. From the graph, $x > 0$.

Using the GDC, we find that when $y = 1$, $x = 1$; and when $y = 77$, $x = 5$.

So the domain is $1 \le x < 5$.

3. (a)

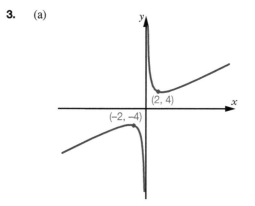

(b)

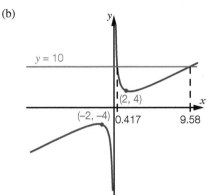

From GDC, when $y = 10$, $x = 0.417$ or 9.58

(c)

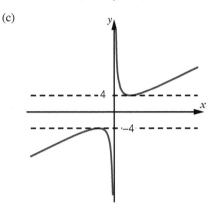

From the graph, the equation has one solution when k is the y-coordinate of a stationary point; that is, $k = -4$ or 4.

4. When $x = 0$, $y = 5$,

so $5 = a + b \times 2^0 \Rightarrow a + b = 5$ $\cdots$ (1)

When $x = 1$, $y = 8$,

so $8 = a + b \times 2^1 \Rightarrow a + 2b = 8$ $\cdots$ (2)

Solving (1) and (2) simultaneously gives $a = 2$, $b = 3$.

5. $g(x) = x^3 - ax + b \Rightarrow g'(x) = 3x^2 - a$

$g(2) = -2 \Rightarrow 2^3 - 2a + b = -2$
$\Rightarrow 2a - b = 10$
$g'(2) = 3 \Rightarrow 3 \times 2^2 - a = 3$
$\Rightarrow a = 9$

Substituting $a = 9$ into the first equation gives $18 - b = 10$, so $b = 8$.

10 DIFFERENTIATION

Mixed practice 10

1. (a) $f(x) = x^2 + \dfrac{3}{x} = x^2 + 3x^{-1}$

$\Rightarrow f'(x) = 2x - 3x^{-2} = 2x - \dfrac{3}{x^2}$

(b) The gradient of the tangent at the point where $x = 3$ is

$f'(3) = 2 \times 3 - \dfrac{3}{3^2} = \dfrac{17}{3}$

2. Method 1: The function is decreasing when $f'(x) < 0$.

$f'(x) < 0$
$\Rightarrow 6x + 4 < 0$
$\Rightarrow x < -\dfrac{2}{3}$

Method 2: Sketch the graph using the GDC.

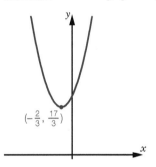

The function is decreasing to the left of the minimum point, i.e. for $x < -\dfrac{2}{3}$

3. $\dfrac{dy}{dx} = 2x - 6$
$2x - 6 = 4 \Rightarrow x = 5$

When $x = 5$, $y = 5^2 - 6 \times 5 + 5 = 25 - 30 + 5 = 0$

So the coordinates are $(5, 0)$.

4. $y = x^3 - 6x \Rightarrow \dfrac{dy}{dx} = 3x^2 - 6$

Tangent(s) will be parallel to $y = 21x + 4$ when

$\dfrac{dy}{dx} = 21$, i.e. when

$3x^2 - 6 = 21$
$3x^2 = 27$
$x = \pm 3$

$x = 3 \Rightarrow y = 3^3 - 6 \times 3 = 9$. So equation of the tangent at $(3, 9)$ is

$y - y_1 = m(x - x_1)$
$y - 9 = 21(x - 3)$
$y = 21x - 54$

$x = -3 \Rightarrow y = (-3)^3 - 6 \times (-3) = -9$. So equation of the tangent at $(-3, -9)$ is

$$y - y_1 = m(x - x_1)$$
$$y + 9 = 21(x + 3)$$
$$y = 21x + 54$$

5. $y = ax^2 + 4x + b \Rightarrow \dfrac{dy}{dx} = 2ax + 4$

Since the gradient of the tangent at $x = 2$ is 24, we have
$2a(2) + 4 = 24$

$\therefore a = 5$

Substituting $x = 2$ into the equation of the tangent:

$$y = 24(2) - 23 = 25$$

So the point $(2, 25)$ lies on the original curve. Therefore,

$$25 = a(2)^2 + 4(2) + b$$
$$25 = 5(4) + 8 + b \qquad \text{(since } a = 5\text{)}$$
$$\therefore b = -3$$

6. (a) The time of initial planting corresponds to $t = 0$. When $t = 0$, $h = 12$, so the height was $12\,\text{cm}$.

(b) When $t = 3$, $h = 3^2 + 3^3 + 12 = 48$, so the height is $48\,\text{cm}$.

(c) The rate of change of the height is $\dfrac{dh}{dt} = 2t + 3t^2$.
When $t = 3$, $\dfrac{dh}{dt} = 2(3) + 3(3)^2 = 33$, so the rate of increase is $33\,\text{cm}$ per day.

7. (a) $f(2) = 4(2)^4 - \dfrac{1}{2(2)} + 5 = \dfrac{275}{4} = 68.75$

(b) $f(x) = 4x^4 - \dfrac{1}{2x} + 5 = 4x^4 - \dfrac{1}{2}x^{-1} + 5$

$\Rightarrow f'(x) = 16x^3 + \dfrac{1}{2}x^{-2} = 16x^3 + \dfrac{1}{2x^2}$

$\therefore f'(2) = 16(2)^3 + \dfrac{1}{2 \times 2^2} = \dfrac{1025}{8} = 128.125$

(c) The gradient of the normal is $m = -\dfrac{8}{1025}$

$= -0.00780$

Therefore, the equation of the normal at $(2, 68.75)$ is

$$y - y_1 = m(x - x_1)$$
$$y - 68.75 = -0.00780(x - 2)$$
$$y = -0.00780x + 68.8$$

8. $y = x^3 - 12x + 4 \Rightarrow \dfrac{dy}{dx} = 3x^2 - 12$

Any tangent parallel to the x-axis has gradient 0:
$3x^2 - 12 = 0$

$\Leftrightarrow x = \pm 2$

When $x = 2$, $y = 2^3 - 12 \times 2 + 4 = 8 - 24 + 4 = -12$
When $x = -2$, $y = (-2)^3 - 12(-2) + 4 = -8 + 24 + 4 = 20$
So the coordinates are $(2, -12)$ and $(-2, 20)$.

9. (a) Surface area $= 2x^2 + 4xy$

$\therefore 100 = 2x^2 + 4xy$

$\Rightarrow 4xy = 100 - 2x^2$

$\Rightarrow y = \dfrac{100 - 2x^2}{4x}$

$= \dfrac{100}{4x} - \dfrac{2x^2}{4x}$

$= \dfrac{25}{x} - \dfrac{x}{2}$

(b) Volume $= x^2 y$

$= x^2 \left(\dfrac{25}{x} - \dfrac{x}{2} \right)$

$= \dfrac{25x^2}{x} - \dfrac{x^3}{2}$

$= 25x - \dfrac{x^3}{2}$

(c) <u>Method 1</u>: Draw the graph of $V = 25x - \dfrac{x^3}{2}$ on the GDC and find the coordinates of the maximum point.

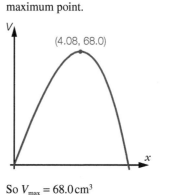

So $V_{\text{max}} = 68.0\,\text{cm}^3$

<u>Method 2</u>: $V = 25x - \dfrac{x^3}{2} \Rightarrow \dfrac{dV}{dx} = 25 - \dfrac{3}{2}x^2$

The maximum point has $\dfrac{dV}{dx} = 0$:

$25 - \dfrac{3x^2}{2} = 0$

$\Leftrightarrow 3x^2 = 50$

$\therefore x = 4.08 \quad (x > 0)$

Substituting $x = 4.08$ into the expression for V gives $V = 68.0\,\text{cm}^3$.

10. (a) $f'(x) = 6x^2 - 18x + 12$

(b) $f'(x) = 0$

$\Leftrightarrow 6x^2 - 18x + 12 = 0$

$\Leftrightarrow x^2 - 3x + 2 = 0$

$\Leftrightarrow (x - 1)(x - 2) = 0$

$\Leftrightarrow x = 1 \text{ or } 2$

(c) Stationary points occur when $f'(x) = 0$, and we know from part (b) that this happens when $x = 1$ or $x = 2$.

$f(1) = 2 - 9 + 12 + 5 = 10$

$f(2) = 2(2)^3 - 9(2)^2 + 12(2) + 5 = 9$

Hence, the coordinates are (1, 10) and (2, 9).

(d)

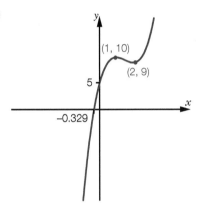

(e) From the graph, $f(x)$ is increasing for: $x < 1$ and $x > 2$.

11. (a) $f(1) = a + \dfrac{1}{2} + 5$

(b) $f(x) = ax + \dfrac{1}{2x} + 5 = ax + \dfrac{1}{2}x^{-1} + 5$

$\Rightarrow f'(x) = a - \dfrac{1}{2}x^{-2} = a - \dfrac{1}{2x^2}$

(c) The gradient of tangent at $x = 1$ is $f'(1)$. So

$a - \dfrac{1}{2 \times 1^2} = \dfrac{7}{2}$

$\Leftrightarrow a = 4$

(d) (i) Gradient of the normal is $m = -\dfrac{2}{7}$.

So, when $x = 1$, $y = a + \dfrac{1}{2} + 5 = \dfrac{19}{2}$

Equation of the normal at $\left(1, \dfrac{19}{2}\right)$ is

$y - y_1 = m(x - x_1)$

$y - \dfrac{19}{2} = -\dfrac{2}{7}(x - 1)$

$14y - 133 = -4x + 4$

$14y + 4x = 137$

(ii) To find the points of intersection, solve the simultaneous equations

$$\begin{cases} y = 4x + \dfrac{1}{2x} + 5 \\ 14y + 4x = 137 \end{cases}$$

From GDC, the intersections are at (1, 9.5) and (0.117, 9.75). The first point is the one found in part (d)(i), so the normal meets the curve again at (0.117, 9.75).

(e)

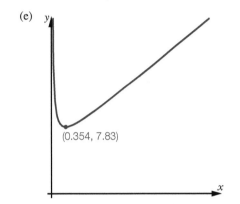

(f) From GDC, the minimum point is (0.354, 7.83).

(g) From graph, $f(x)$ is decreasing for $0 < x < 0.354$.

Going for the top 10

1. $y = ax^2 + bx + 4 \Rightarrow \dfrac{dy}{dx} = 2ax + b$

A maximum point has $\dfrac{dy}{dx} = 0$, so we know that

when $x = 4$, $\dfrac{dy}{dx} = 0$:

$2a \times 4 + b = 0$

$\therefore 8a + b = 0 \quad \cdots (1)$

Since the curve passes through the point with coordinates $x = 4$, $y = 8$:

$8 = a \times 4^2 + b \times 4 + 4$

$\therefore 16a + 4b = 4 \quad \cdots (2)$

Solving equations (1) and (2) simultaneously (e.g. by using the GDC) gives $a = -0.25$, $b = 2$.

2. $y = ax^3 + 3x + b \Rightarrow \dfrac{dy}{dx} = 3ax^2 + 3$

The gradient of the tangent at $x = 1$ is $\dfrac{dy}{dx}$ evaluated at

$x = 1$, and we know that this is 15. So

$3a \times 1^2 + 3 = 15$

$\Rightarrow a = 4$

Using the equation of the tangent, we find that when $x = 1$, $y = 15(1) - 2 = 13$, so the curve passes through (1, 13). Therefore, substituting these coordinates into the equation of the curve gives

$13 = 4 \times 1^3 + 3 \times 1 + b$

$\Rightarrow b = 6$

3. Sketch the graph using the GDC:

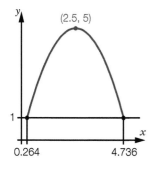

(a) For both Jane and Hilary, $y = 1$.

From the graph, the intersections of the curve with the line $y = 1$ occur at $x = 0.2639$ and $x = 4.7361$, so these are the positions of Jane and Hilary.

Therefore, the distance between them is $4.7361 - 0.2639 = 4.47\,\text{m}$ (3 SF).

(b) We can use the GDC to find the y-coordinate of the maximum point.

Alternatively, use differentiation to find the stationary point:

$y = 4x - 0.8x^2 \Rightarrow \dfrac{dy}{dx} = 4 - 1.6x$

$\dfrac{dy}{dx} = 0 \Leftrightarrow 4 - 1.6x \Leftrightarrow x = 2.5$

and at this point, $y = 4 \times 2.5 - 0.8(2.5)^2 = 5$

So the maximum height that the ball reaches is $5\,\text{m}$.

ANSWERS TO PRACTICE QUESTIONS

1 WORKING WITH NUMBERS

1.

	$\mathbb{N}$	$\mathbb{Z}$	$\mathbb{Q}$	$\mathbb{R}$
-3	✗	✓	✓	✓
0.76	✗	✗	✓	✓
$\cos 120°$	✗	✗	✓	✓
$\sqrt{5}$	✗	✗	✗	✓
1.23×10^8	✓	✓	✓	✓

2.

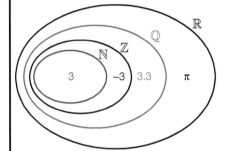

3. (a) 0.6 (b) 1

4. (a) 8.96×10^6 (b) 3.5×10^{14}

5. $1.22 \times 10^2\,\text{kg/s}$

6. (a) $13.6\,\text{m}^2$ (b) $136\,000\,\text{cm}^2$

   (c) $1.36 \times 10^5\,\text{cm}^2$

7. (a) 3.142 (b) 0.0130%

8. (a) 6.78; 3.14 (b) 2354.151931

   (c) 2339.823044 (d) 1 SF

   (e) 0.609%

9. 0.633; 607.59 GBP

10. (a) 495.48 SAR (b) 0.905%

2 SEQUENCES AND SERIES

1. (a) 53 (b) 490

2. (a) 3.5 (b) 17th

   (c) 13 or 20

3. (a) 2560 (b) 5120

   (c) 20475

4. (a) $r = 4$, $u_1 = 0.5$

   (b) 9th (c) 10

5. $r = 4$

6. (a) €8,748 (b) 14

7. (a) ¥7465 (b) ¥7960

8. $337.46

3 DESCRIPTIVE STATISTICS

1. (a) The values are already arranged in order and there are 13 of them, so the median is the 7th number. The lower quartile is therefore the median of the first six numbers, which is the mean of the 3rd and 4th numbers, i.e. the mean of 5 and 10.

   (b) 14.5

2. $x = 2$

3. Median = 5, IQR = 2

4. (a) $k = 1$ (b) 1.38

5. (a) $x = 6$, $y = 7$ (b) $2.21\,\text{m}$

6. (a) Lower: $23.5\,\text{m}$; upper: $29.5\,\text{m}$

   (b)

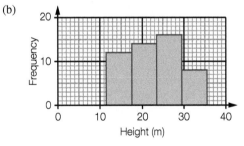

   (c) Mean $22.9\,\text{m}$, standard deviation $6.12\,\text{m}$

7. (a) Lower: 21; upper: 31; mid-interval value 26

   (b)

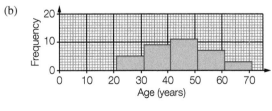

   (c) Mean 44.3 years, standard deviation 11.6 years

8. (a) 59

(b)
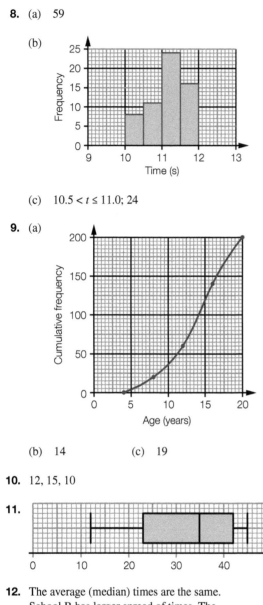

(c) $10.5 < t \le 11.0$; 24

9. (a)

(b) 14   (c) 19

10. 12, 15, 10

11.

12. The average (median) times are the same. School B has larger spread of times. The distribution of times for school B is more symmetrical.

4 SET THEORY AND VENN DIAGRAMS

1. (a) {1, 2, 4, 5, 10}   (b) {2, 4, 10}

(c) {1, 3, 5, 6, 7, 8, 9}

2. (c) and (d)

3. (a), (b) and (c)

4.
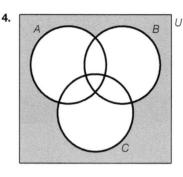

5.
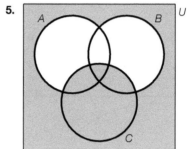

6. $(A \cap B') \cup C$

7. 9

8. 15

9. (a) 7   (b) 6

5 LOGIC

1.

p	q	r	q∨r	p∧(q∨r)
T	T	T	T	T
T	T	F	T	T
T	F	T	T	T
T	F	F	F	F
F	T	T	T	F
F	T	F	T	F
F	F	T	T	F
F	F	F	F	F

7. (a) (i) $p \wedge \neg q$ (ii) $p \Rightarrow q$

(b) There are puddles and rain if and only if I am wearing a raincoat.

8. (a) If you are happy then you are smiling.

(b) If you are not smiling then you are not happy.

(c) If you are not happy then you are not smiling.

9. A

10. (a) Valid; every natural number is also a real number.

   (b) Valid; if a number is real and rational, it is also real.

   (c) Not valid; if a number is real but not rational (i.e. it is irrational), then it is not a natural number (for example, π).

6 PROBABILITY

1. (a) $\dfrac{2}{11}$ (b) $\dfrac{2}{110} = \dfrac{1}{55}$ (c) $\dfrac{1}{4}$

2. (a) $\dfrac{13}{50} = 0.26$ (b) $\dfrac{13}{25} = 0.52$

3. (a)

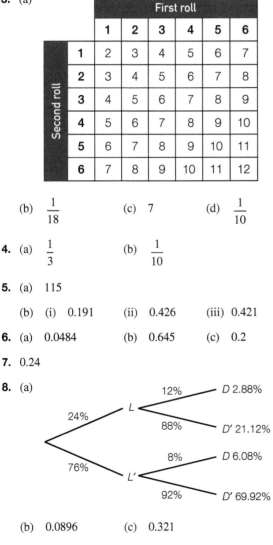

		First roll					
		1	**2**	**3**	**4**	**5**	**6**
Second roll	**1**	2	3	4	5	6	7
	2	3	4	5	6	7	8
	3	4	5	6	7	8	9
	4	5	6	7	8	9	10
	5	6	7	8	9	10	11
	6	7	8	9	10	11	12

   (b) $\dfrac{1}{18}$ (c) 7   (d) $\dfrac{1}{10}$

4. (a) $\dfrac{1}{3}$ (b) $\dfrac{1}{10}$

5. (a) 115

   (b) (i) 0.191   (ii) 0.426   (iii) 0.421

6. (a) 0.0484   (b) 0.645   (c) 0.2

7. 0.24

8. (a)

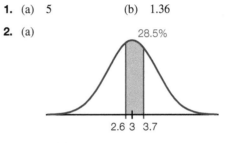

   (b) 0.0896   (c) 0.321

9. (a)

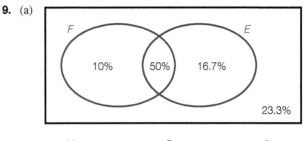

   (b) (i) $\dfrac{23}{30} = 76.7\%$ (ii) $\dfrac{7}{30} = 23.3\%$ (iii) $\dfrac{3}{4}$

10. (a) 0.4   (b) 0.5

7 STATISTICAL APPLICATIONS

1. (a) 5   (b) 1.36

2. (a)

28.5%

2.6 3 3.7

   (b) 5.06

3. $r = -0.355$. There is no correlation between the two sets of marks.

4. (a) Jack's interpretation is correct; there is strong positive correlation between the a person's salary and the value of their car.

   (b) Jill's interpretation is wrong; correlation does not imply causation.

5. (a) $y = 0.0710x + 0.116$ (b) 5.69

6. (a) (i) 39 000

   (ii) Not reliable because $A = 56$ is outside the range of the data.

   (b) Not reliable because the correlation coefficient is close to 0 and so a linear model is not appropriate.

7. (a) H_0: Favourite colour is independent of gender.

   H_1: Favourite colour is dependent on gender.

   (b) Expected frequencies:

	Red	Blue	Green
Boy	21.3	21.3	14.5
Girl	22.7	22.7	15.5

   $\chi^2 = 9.89$, $p = 7.10 \times 10^{-3}$

   (c) Reject H_0; p-value is less than significance level 10%.

8. (a) H_0: The length of a dog's tail is independent of its colour.

  H_1: The length of a dog's tail is related to its colour.

 (b) 2

 (c) Do not reject H_0; there is not sufficient evidence that the length of a dog's tail is related to its colour.

9. (a) $A = 115, B = 58, C = 17, D = 14$

 (b) $\dfrac{58 \times 88}{270} = 18.9$

 (c) $\chi^2 = 57.9 > 9.48$. Reject H_0; there is evidence that the favourite subject is not independent of first language.

8 GEOMETRY AND TRIGONOMETRY

1. $y = \dfrac{3}{2}x + \dfrac{1}{2}$ or $3x - 2y + 1 = 0$

2. (a) $y = \dfrac{1}{2}x - 5$

 (b) Yes; gradient of l_2 is -2, and $-2 \times \dfrac{1}{2} = -1$, so the lines are perpendicular.

3. $66.0°$

4. (a) 754 m   (b) 78.8 m

5. (a) $\dfrac{6 + \sqrt{120}}{2} \approx 8.48$ (b) $39.0°$

6. (a) 22.1 m   (b) 28.3 m

7. (a) $48.9°$ (b) 9.49 cm

8. (a) $21.4°$ (b) 14.7 cm   (c) $29.5\,\text{cm}^2$

9. (a) $110°$; 11.0 cm (b) 46.8 cm

10. (a)

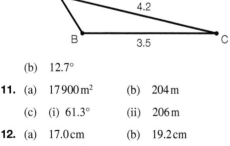

 (b) $12.7°$

11. (a) $17\,900\,\text{m}^2$ (b) 204 m

 (c) (i) $61.3°$ (ii) 206 m

12. (a) 17.0 cm   (b) 19.2 cm

 (c) (i) $33.2°$ (ii) $66.2°$

13. (a) (i) 22.2 cm   (ii) 23.3 cm

 (b) $17.5°$ (c) $72.5°$

14. (a) 8.66 cm   (b) 23.5 cm

 (c) $90°$ (d) $20.2°$

15. (a) 22.0 m

 (b) (i) $48.2°$ (ii) $35.3°$

16. $417\,\text{cm}^2$

17. (a) $9\pi r^2\,\text{cm}^2$ (b) 2   (c) $92.2\,\text{cm}^3$

18. (a) 4.40 cm   (b) $934\,\text{cm}^2$

19. (a) $132\,\text{cm}^3$ (b) 7.21 cm; $213\,\text{cm}^2$

9 FUNCTIONS, EQUATIONS AND MATHEMATICAL MODELS

1. $x = -1.23, 0.460$

2. $x = -2.46, -0.239, 1.70$

3. 1.53

4. $A = 5, k = 1$

5. $x = 5.61, y = 2.46$

6. $u_1 = 13, d = 3$

7. $a = 0.0208, b = 20.3$

8. (a) $26r + 42b = 272$

 (b) 1.35 dollars

9. Domain: $x \in \mathbb{R}, x \neq -2$; range: $y \in \mathbb{R}, y \neq 4$

10. $y \geq 3$

11. (a) Domain: $\{1, 5, 6, 8, 12\}$; range: $\{1, 3, 5\}$

 (b) $x = 5$ or 8

12. (a) $m = 2.8 + 0.15n$

 (b) 3.4 kg   (c) 8 weeks

13. More than 200 texts

14. (a) $C_1(d) = 2.4 + 1.2d, C_2(d) = 1.65d$

 (b) 6

15. (a) $x(a - x); x = 0, a$

 (b) $a = 4$ (c) 4 m

16. (a) $t = \dfrac{k}{9.8}$ (b) $k = 19.8$

 (c) 0.532 s and 1.92 s

17. (a) $b = 2, c = -3$ (b) $(-1, -4)$

18. (a) B   (b) A   (c) C

19. (a) $c = 2, k = 4$ (b) $2.16 < y < 102$

20. (a) 66° (b) 16°
(c) 19.1° (d) 0.529 minutes or 31.8 seconds

21. (a) $c = -11, k = 7$ (b) 45

22. (a) 4.20, 3.04, 2.07, 1.39, 1.10, 1.39

(b)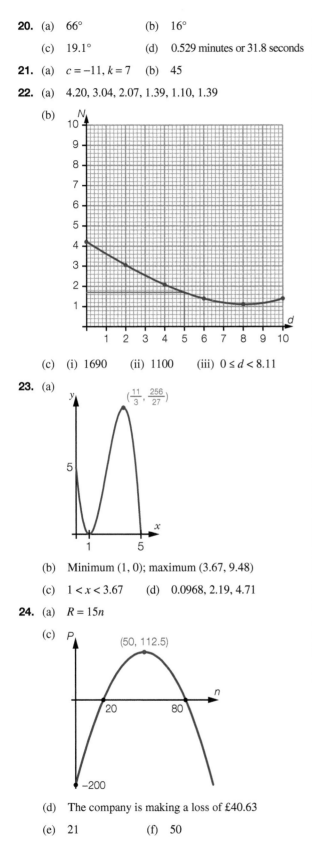

(c) (i) 1690 (ii) 1100 (iii) $0 \le d < 8.11$

23. (a)

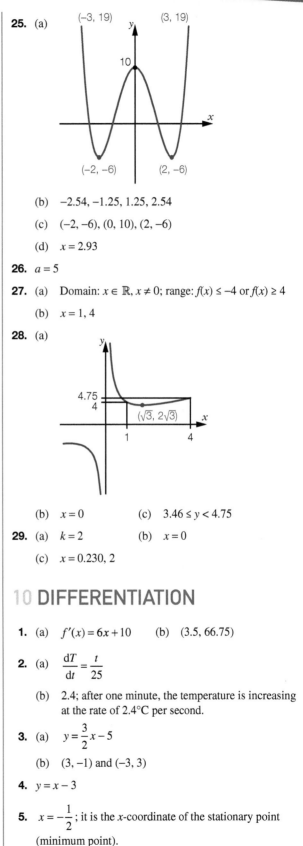

(b) Minimum (1, 0); maximum (3.67, 9.48)
(c) $1 < x < 3.67$ (d) 0.0968, 2.19, 4.71

24. (a) $R = 15n$
(c)

(d) The company is making a loss of £40.63
(e) 21 (f) 50

25. (a)

(b) $-2.54, -1.25, 1.25, 2.54$
(c) $(-2, -6), (0, 10), (2, -6)$
(d) $x = 2.93$

26. $a = 5$

27. (a) Domain: $x \in \mathbb{R}, x \ne 0$; range: $f(x) \le -4$ or $f(x) \ge 4$
(b) $x = 1, 4$

28. (a)

(b) $x = 0$ (c) $3.46 \le y < 4.75$

29. (a) $k = 2$ (b) $x = 0$
(c) $x = 0.230, 2$

10 DIFFERENTIATION

1. (a) $f'(x) = 6x + 10$ (b) (3.5, 66.75)

2. (a) $\dfrac{\mathrm{d}T}{\mathrm{d}t} = \dfrac{t}{25}$

(b) 2.4; after one minute, the temperature is increasing at the rate of 2.4°C per second.

3. (a) $y = \dfrac{3}{2}x - 5$

(b) (3, −1) and (−3, 3)

4. $y = x - 3$

5. $x = -\dfrac{1}{2}$; it is the x-coordinate of the stationary point (minimum point).

6. (a)

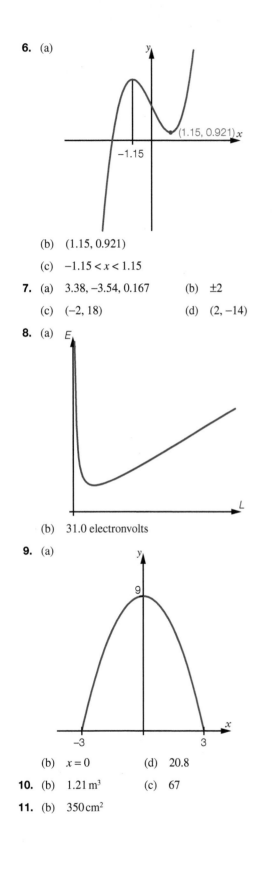

(1.15, 0.921) x

−1.15

(b) (1.15, 0.921)

(c) −1.15 < x < 1.15

7. (a) 3.38, −3.54, 0.167 (b) ±2

(c) (−2, 18) (d) (2, −14)

8. (a) E

L

(b) 31.0 electronvolts

9. (a) y

9

−3 3 x

(b) $x = 0$ (d) 20.8

10. (b) 1.21 m³ (c) 67

11. (b) 350 cm²

11 EXAMINATION SUPPORT

Spot the common errors

1. Only the number 2 should be raised to the power 4; the correct answer is $3 \times 16 = 48$

2. Sign error in multiplying out the bracket $(n - 1)(-3)$; it should become $-3n + 3$

3. The exponent is '$2x$'; must put brackets around it when entering into the GDC

4. $\dfrac{1}{3x} = \dfrac{1}{3}x^{-1}$ not $3x^{-1}$

5. Incorrect expansion of $(x - 3)^2$; it should be $(x - 3)(x - 3) = x^2 - 6x + 9$

6. (a) Need to square the negative number −5; must use brackets

   (b) The exponent is the whole of '$1.02 + 3.07$'; must put brackets around it

   (c) Need to take the square root of the entire expression '$4.2 - 1.7$'; must use brackets